'Trystan Owain Hughes offer
through to Easter, drawing on literature, theology, scripture
and easily appreciated events from his own daily life and
the lives of others. I thank him for the work he has done
to provide such an accessible, stimulating and refreshing
resource.'
John Davies, archbishop of Wales

'Using a rich blend of story, insight and commentary,
Trystan guides us on a Lenten journey of grace. As he
encourages us to open ourselves to God and his loving
kingdom, he gently challenges us to yield to the One who
loves us. Sign up to the journey – you won't regret it!'
Amy Boucher Pye, author of *The Living Cross*

'These rich, accessible reflections are full of stories, insight,
humour and wisdom that will enable you to truly open your
eyes and heart to what God is doing around you as you
explore the strange gifts that the disciplines of Lent bring.'
Graham Tomlin, bishop of Kensington

The Bible Reading Fellowship
15 The Chambers, Vineyard
Abingdon OX14 3FE
brf.org.uk

The Bible Reading Fellowship (BRF) is a Registered Charity (233280)

ISBN 978 0 85746 882 6
First published 2020
10 9 8 7 6 5 4 3 2 1 0
All rights reserved

Text © Trystan Owain Hughes 2020
This edition © The Bible Reading Fellowship 2020
Cover image © Lightstock

The author asserts the moral right to be identified as the author of this work

Acknowledgements
Scripture quotations are taken from The Holy Bible, New International Version
(Anglicised edition) copyright © 1979, 1984, 2011 by Biblica. Used by permission of
Hodder & Stoughton Publishers, a Hachette UK company. All rights reserved. 'NIV'
is a registered trademark of Biblica. UK trademark number 1448790.

'Ideology' words and music by Billy Bragg © 1986. Reproduced by permission of
Sony/ATV Music Publishing (UK) Ltd, London W1T 3LP.

Every effort has been made to trace and contact copyright owners for material
used in this resource. We apologise for any inadvertent omissions or errors, and
would ask those concerned to contact us so that full acknowledgement can be
made in the future.

A catalogue record for this book is available from the British Library

Printed and bound by CPI Group (UK) Ltd, Croydon CR0 4YY

TRYSTAN ØWAIN HUGHES

OPENING OUR LIVES

Devotional readings for Lent

Contents

WEEK 3: OPEN OUR HEARTS TO YOUR LOVE

WEEK 4: OPEN OUR WAYS TO YOUR WILL

WEEK 5: OPEN OUR ACTIONS TO YOUR COMPASSION

Contents

HOLY WEEK: OPEN OUR PAIN TO YOUR PEACE

CONCLUSION: OPEN OUR WORLD TO YOUR HOPE

Acknowledgements

Thank you to my friends and family who have supported my writing down the years, and to all who have written kind emails, social media messages and letters of support after reading my books. Your enthusiasm, love and support have made the process of writing even more worthwhile.

A huge and special thank you to Jenny Wigley, Sue and Bruce Hurrell and my wife Sandra for their many wise suggestions after they faithfully and diligently read every chapter.

Thank you also to the following for advice, support, and assistance with stories: Kath and Mike Lawley, Archbishop Barry Morgan, Bishop David Wilbourne, Sameh Otri, Paul Francis, Chris Burr, Haydn and Gill, Colin and Ann, Janice Brown, Perry Buck, Siôn Brynach, Pamela Day, Greg Dixon, Dominic de Saulles, Keith Hebden, Ethan Hall, Alex Kinsey, Linda Alexandra, Sylvia McCarty, Judith Hill, Jeremy Duff, Gaz Roberts, Eleanor Williams, Billy Bragg and Paul Fitzpatrick.

Thank you to Bishop June Osborne for supporting my ministry.

Thank you to everyone at BRF for believing others would find my thoughts and reflections worthwhile reading. A big *diolch* to my ever-supportive family in north Wales, especially to my mum and dad and to my siblings, Marc, Angharad, Dyfan and Gwynan, and their families.

Finally, a big *danke schön* to my wonderful family – to Lukas, Lena and Macsen – for providing countless illustrations for sermons, books and talks down the years and for continuing to bring so much fun and laughter into my life, and especially to my wonderful, beautiful and talented wife, Sandra, for being my very best friend – *ich liebe dich*.

Introduction

Beginning the journey

The kingdom invitation

One spring morning a number of years back, I went for a coffee with a friend of mine, the Muslim chaplain to our local university. As we sat down in a cafe that serves the tastiest cakes, he said to me, 'Oh, no! I've just remembered: it's Lent for you, isn't it? So you must be fasting and can't eat anything.' I explained to him that, for Christians, fasting during Lent differed from fasting for Muslims during Ramadan. Many Christians, I continued, simply give up something specific, like chocolate, cakes or sweets. 'Ah, I understand now,' he said, as he chose a big slice of cake. 'So what did you give up?' 'Oh, no,' I quickly replied. 'What I meant was that *other* Christians give up something during Lent. I haven't given anything up and so can eat as much cake as I want.'

While we laughed together over our cakes, this conversation stayed with me. More than simply inspiring me to begin to give up something each Lent (which it did), it also led me to start thinking about how Christians in the 21st century could be challenged in a different way through the discipline of the Lenten period. In our hectic schedules, with all the demands and duties that we face today, perhaps the 40 days of Lent can offer a first step towards a fresh way of approaching our faith.

The practice of giving up something over Lent is, of course, an ancient tradition. Soon after the gospels were written, there is evidence that Christians would go without food or drink for 40 hours, between Good Friday afternoon and Easter morning. By the fifth century, and possibly earlier, fasting had been extended to the whole Lenten season. Today, many of us still feast on pancakes on Shrove Tuesday, even if we are not then giving up sugary and rich food for Lent, as was the traditional practice. Self-discipline and self-control are important in the Christian life, so giving up anything, even something as innocuous as chocolate, can be a spiritual practice and can thus bring us closer to God.

In recent years, though, Christians have begun to be more creative about Lenten disciplines. Rather than *giving up*, some have embraced *giving to* a charity each day (or week) over Lent. Others have championed *taking up* over giving up, by committing to carrying out acts of compassion or kindness each day. Churches and denominations are now using Lent to inspire and support important causes through giving up, giving to and taking up. Recently, for example, the Church of England has encouraged awareness of climate change through Lenten discipline. In 2018, it distributed a calendar with environmentally themed Bible verses and suggestions on avoiding single-use plastics. A year later, it encouraged worshippers to go on 'litter pilgrimages', in which they were to walk together, pray together and collect rubbish strewn on our streets. Similarly, the charity Stewardship's popular 40acts challenge urges Christians to view Lent as a time of radical generosity as well as spiritual discipline, with individuals and groups signing up to emails which detail daily challenges through the 40 days, including compassionate actions, environmental steps and charitable giving, and then being encouraged to share their efforts on social media.

Whether you intend to give up, give to or take up, this book adds another dimension – encouraging you also to *open up* this Lent. Each week you will be invited to open up to different ways of experiencing the kingdom of God, being challenged to think and reflect on biblical passages and, by so doing, open each part of your life to God's Spirit.

Many churches worldwide celebrate Jesus' kingship prior to Advent, with a Sunday dedicated to Christ the King. This festival has been placed, very deliberately, at the end of the liturgical year, to root the kingship of Jesus in the future, as we await his coming kingdom. This Lent, though, we are going to be encouraged to recognise that

Christ's kingdom is in the *now* as well as being *not yet*. Jesus, after all, is already our king, and although we will witness his kingdom in its fullness in the future, it is already here. Our invitation is now to open ourselves to recognising that kingdom's beauty, wonder, comfort and love all around us. Once you have opened yourself up in this way for the Lenten period, the challenge will then be to continue seeing, hearing and living out God's kingdom beyond Easter.

Our Lenten prayer

Before you read each daily reflection, calm your heart and mind by slowly reading, or saying out loud, the following prayer:

Loving God,
in our sufferings and joys,
in our relationships and daily lives,
we ask that your kingdom come.
Open our eyes to your presence,
open our ears to your call,
open our hearts to your love,
open our ways to your will,
open our actions to your compassion,
open our pain to your peace,
and, in doing so, open our world to your hope.
In the name of Jesus,
Amen

=== **WEEK 1** ===

Open our eyes to your presence

Ash Wednesday

Like salt in water

Surely I was sinful at birth,
  sinful from the time my mother conceived me.
Yet you desired faithfulness even in the womb;
  you taught me wisdom in that secret place.
Cleanse me with hyssop, and I shall be clean;
  wash me, and I shall be whiter than snow.
Let me hear joy and gladness;
  let the bones you have crushed rejoice.
Hide your face from my sins
  and blot out all my iniquity.
Create in me a pure heart, O God,
  and renew a steadfast spirit within me.
Do not cast me from your presence
  or take your Holy Spirit from me.
Restore to me the joy of your salvation
  and grant me a willing spirit, to sustain me.

PSALM 51:5–12

Ash Wednesday, the first day of Lent, is a day of repentance. Traditionally, it is a day when Christians ask for forgiveness for past actions that have caused hurt and pain. As a result, God grants us a new start, or, in the words of the psalmist in today's passage, a pure heart and a steadfast spirit. Yet it has been tempting for Christians down the years to regard the day as the beginning of a time in which we reject worldly joys and embrace sombre asceticism – the beginning of discipline and denial, where spirit conquers flesh. After all, the 40 days of Lent recall Jesus' time of prayer and fasting in the unforgiving Palestinian wilderness.

In his poem 'Ash Wednesday', T.S. Eliot suggests that the stark split between world and spirit is a misunderstanding of Ash Wednesday. Instead, Eliot had become convinced that accepting the Word of God in his life meant appreciating creation, not rejecting it. Ash Wednesday is certainly a time of repentance, but we don't only ask forgiveness for the things we've done; we also ask forgiveness for the things we haven't done. And this leads us, according to Eliot, to ask forgiveness for the times when we so often walk blindly past God's wonderful creation without truly appreciating his presence.

Even the ash that is put on foreheads today is a reminder of this. Traditionally, the ash is a reminder of our mortality – 'From dust we come and to dust we shall return,' as the Ash Wednesday liturgy puts it. But it also reminds us of the interconnectedness of the world around us. After all, there are few things more earthy than ash. As such, it can help us to open our eyes to an appreciation of the wonder and beauty of the world around us. As Thomas Merton put it, Ash Wednesday is the beginning of 'realizing what we had perhaps not seen before; the light of Lent is given us to help us with this realization'. No wonder the psalmist in today's passage speaks of joy and gladness.

There is an old story from India about a young boy who told his father that he'd decided that there was no God, as he could not see any evidence of his presence. The father told his son to find a bowl of water and some salt. On his return, he asked his son to pour the salt into the water, stir it and leave it overnight. The next day, the father asked the son to bring him the salt that he had put in the water. The salt, of course, had dissolved, so the son was unable to fulfil his father's request. His dad, therefore, ordered him to sip from the bowl and then asked him how it tasted. 'Salty,' the boy answered. He then told his son to throw the water on the floor. The next day the father took him back to where the water had been thrown. The water had by then evaporated, and the salt had reappeared. 'Like salt in water,' the dad concluded, 'we may not be able see God directly in our world, but he is here.'

God does not always reveal himself to us in an obvious way. Rather, like salt in water, we need to taste him and recognise him all around us. He is in the moments of love, beauty and joy that touch us each day, and, whenever we experience these things, we experience him. Once we start to recognise the divine in the midst of our everyday lives, we will start to realise that Jesus is walking alongside us on our journeys. We just need to open our eyes to discover his presence around us.

In some monasteries on Ash Wednesday, the monks receive the ashes barefoot, so they can remind themselves of their intimate connection with the world beneath their feet. Our world is, after all, steeped in God's presence, dripping in his glory and beauty. Our invitation is to open our eyes to this fact – to the daffodils and snowdrops that are beginning to appear in our parks, to the squirrels which dash in front of us, to the smile of a shop assistant who gives us our change, to the phone conversation with an old school friend, to the memories of times or people now long gone, to the uplifting music on the radio, to the laughter of children in the playground and to the stillness of silence.

Thomas Merton asserted that the cross is traced upon our foreheads on Ash Wednesday not as a 'sacrament of death', but as a sign of life. After all, today we embark on a journey that does not end with the crucifixion, but with an empty cross, with the new life of resurrection. In fact, in many traditions, the ash is itself from last year's burnt palm crosses, which were, of course, themselves the empty crosses of new life. There is, therefore, no more fitting thing today than to commit ourselves to opening our eyes to God's presence this Lent, in the wonder of his creation, in the places we visit and in the people we meet.

Reflection

Repentance and confession, making ourselves right before God, marks the start of the Lenten journey. They can remind us that there are times we take the beauty and joy of our lives for granted, when we ignore or don't notice God's presence, and when we fail to be grateful for the blessings all around us. Take time now to sit in silence to confess those times when you failed to appreciate God's presence in your life, and commit to recognising him in your Lenten journey.

Thursday

Setting off in a different direction

The beginning of the good news about Jesus the Messiah, the Son of God, as it is written in Isaiah the prophet:

'I will send my messenger ahead of you,
    who will prepare your way' –
'a voice of one calling in the wilderness,
"Prepare the way for the Lord,
    make straight paths for him."'

And so John the Baptist appeared in the wilderness, preaching a baptism of repentance for the forgiveness of sins. The whole Judean countryside and all the people of Jerusalem went out to him. Confessing their sins, they were baptised by him in the River Jordan. John wore clothing made of camel's hair, with a leather belt round his waist, and he ate locusts and wild honey. And this was his message: 'After me comes the one more powerful than I, the straps of whose sandals I am not worthy to stoop down and untie. I baptise you with water, but he will baptise you with the Holy Spirit.'

MARK 1:1–8

A recent study by the TV channel Sky Arts discovered the 40 indicators of being typically British. At number one, unsurprisingly, was 'always talking about the weather'. Following close behind were 'wearing shorts and sunglasses the second the sun comes out' and 'holding the door open for someone who is so far away that they end up running for the door'. In the top ten also, though, was the one that I could really relate to – 'saying sorry too frequently'. My wife's family in Germany don't understand why I have to apologise after almost everything. In fact, when we are visiting Germany, I often end up saying sorry to them for saying sorry so often!

Yesterday, Ash Wednesday allowed us a moment of repentance for those times when we failed to allow God's light to illuminate our lives. The repentance of Lent, though, does not finish there. The Greek word translated as 'repent' in today's passage, *metanoia*, means to stop, turn around and walk the other way. In other words, while repentance does involve remorse for wrongdoing, by recognising that we're going in the wrong direction it also involves turning around to walk towards a life of love, compassion, peace and hope.

In this sense, repentance is far more than a once-in-a-lifetime act, when we decide to follow Jesus and live him out in our daily lives. It is also an act that should happen again and again in our lives. This is related to the theological concept of sanctification (or *theosis* in the Eastern Orthodox Church) and is how the Holy Spirit helps us to grow to be more and more like Jesus himself. We need to be constantly assessing our words, attitudes and actions, and turning again towards living out God's love in our lives. This is one reason why some church traditions take time at the beginning of every service to say a confession – to reflect in silence, to say sorry and to commit to continuing our Christian journey.

That word 'journey' is important here. In today's passage, John the Baptist uses a quotation from the Old Testament prophets that refers to 'the way of the Lord'. That phrase is common in early Jewish writings to express choosing the good but difficult path, as opposed to the wrong but easy road. In fact, Acts 9 tells us that the first followers of Jesus were not called Christians, but known as belonging to 'the Way'. So repentance not only requires much soul-searching and self-awareness, but also much dedication and determination in walking that difficult path. After recognising our shortcomings, it demands that each of us, as followers of 'the Way', commit to becoming more Jesus-like in our words and actions.

While the British excel at apologising for little things, then, this does not necessarily mean that our lives reflect true repentance. In fact, our apologies are all too often superficial and trivial, and rarely transform the way we live. Few of us are good at saying sorry for the things that really matter; even less do we then set off in a different direction. Sorry may well be the hardest word, as Elton John sung, but walking the path of love after that apology is often even harder.

Our human desire to be right makes our journey of transformation particularly difficult. In politics, in the church and on social media, we see an incessant desire to win arguments, despite the fact that, as the broadcaster James O'Brien reminds us, 'winning an argument doesn't necessarily mean we are right'. In our family, we have employed the name of our car's manufacturer, Kia, when any of us are digging our heels in during an argument and refusing to engage with the viewpoint of others – we become a 'Know It All'! Being a Kia, maintaining we alone know best, is all too common in our world and is the first step to lacking humility and to rejecting contrition and change.

God's way demands the difficult step of recognising that none of us are perfect and that our desire to be right leads to a stubbornness of heart that blinds us to our unkindness, self-centredness and thought-lessness. It is only when we embrace *metanoia* that we can set off in a different direction, along a path of love, care and compassion. By doing so, we begin to reflect the light of God's presence in the lives of others and in the world around us.

Reflection

A prayer to be prayed slowly and mindfully – allow each word and phrase to inspire your walk with God:

> Lord of forgiveness,
> you call us to the difficult path of repentance,
> to recognising that we are often walking the wrong way.
> Help us to open our eyes to our failings;
> hold us as we say sorry for times when our thoughts, words or
>   actions go against your love and compassion;
> reassure us of your liberating grace and mercy as we turn around,
>   walk towards your light and reflect your loving presence.
> In Jesus' name,
> Amen

Friday

Not looking, but seeing

The Son is the image of the invisible God, the firstborn over all creation. For in him all things were created: things in heaven and on earth, visible and invisible, whether thrones or powers or rulers or authorities; all things have been created through him and for him. He is before all things, and in him all things hold together. And he is the head of the body, the church; he is the beginning and the firstborn from among the dead, so that in everything he might have the supremacy. For God was pleased to have all his fullness dwell in him, and through him to reconcile to himself all things, whether things on earth or things in heaven, by making peace through his blood, shed on the cross.

COLOSSIANS 1:15–20

When I was growing up, my *taid* (grandfather) used to sit with his little cap on, spitting occasionally into the roaring fire, and tell us stories about his childhood. One of those stories was about the great Welsh revival. It was 1904 and the Holy Spirit was sweeping through Wales like a forest fire. The great revivalist, Evan Roberts, would visit the chapels of Anglesey and preach to the packed buildings for hours. There were reports that, in some chapels, the congregations became so overcome with frenzy at Roberts' words that the Holy Spirit moved them to start dancing around the aisles with joy, and some even got so excited that they began to throw chairs through the windows!

Things are certainly different today. The churches and chapels are still standing on Anglesey, but many are now garages, community centres and supermarkets. The congregations at the buildings that continue to be places of worship are often dwindling and ageing.

I sometimes wonder what the great Welsh Celtic saints would think of the situation today, but perhaps they would not be so disheartened. After all, St David's last words were reputedly *'Cofiwch y pethau bychain'* – 'Remember the small things.' He belonged to a community that recognised the activity of God in every part of life, in even the smallest detail. God, for the Celtic Christians, was to be found in creation, people and places. Echoing the first chapters of Genesis, the Celtic churches continually emphasised that God's creation is good. As a result, they looked for the image of God in all his creation. As our passage today puts it: 'In him all things were created: things in heaven and on earth, visible and invisible… all things have been created through him and for him. He is before all things, and in him all things hold together.' Celtic Christians found God not merely in the stone walls of a church building, but in the local community and the wider world.

It is too easy for Christians to feel downhearted at the state of the church today and, indeed, at the state of the nation or the world. In his parables about the kingdom, though, Jesus challenges us to look beyond what is at the surface. It may look insignificant (a mustard seed, some yeast, a net or a field), but it is something much more precious. As Henry David Thoreau noted: 'The question is not what you look at, but what you see.' Jesus challenges us to open our eyes to the kingdom of God in our everyday lives and to perceive God in our daily existence. God is inextricably woven into our lives and the challenge of our faith is to recognise him each day.

After all, although our passage speaks of an 'invisible God', he is certainly not an absent God. In the BBC comedy *Blackadder Goes Forth*, set during World War I, General Melchett unfurls a map of the battlefield, leans over it and bellows, 'Oh man, it's a barren and featureless desert out there, isn't it?' His assistant, Captain Darling, looks at the blank paper and replies, 'I think you want the other side, sir.' If we open our eyes, we can learn to recognise the other side of this world, woven into our lives – in the beauty of nature, in the friendships we foster and in the kindness we witness. Like the church of St David's time, we can look and expect to find God alive in the community, in our fellow people and in the beauty and wonder of the world around us.

Reflection

The Welsh poet R.S. Thomas reminded us that burning-bush moments of finding God in the tapestry of our lives are like the 'pearl of great price' of Jesus' parable – we should be selling everything to experience them. What does this mean practically in your own life? Have a think about when God's joy and wonder has broken through in your life, perhaps at surprising moments. Finally, commit yourself to looking beyond the surface and to recognising God in the people you meet and the places you visit.

Saturday

God of the in-between times

As Jesus was walking beside the Sea of Galilee, he saw two
brothers, Simon called Peter and his brother Andrew. They
were casting a net into the lake, for they were fishermen.
'Come, follow me,' Jesus said, 'and I will send you out to fish
for people.' At once they left their nets and followed him.
   Going on from there, he saw two other brothers, James son
of Zebedee and his brother John. They were in a boat with
their father Zebedee, preparing their nets. Jesus called them,
and immediately they left the boat and their father and followed him.

MATTHEW 4:18–22

Today's passage describes Jesus calling four of his disciples – Peter,
Andrew, James and John. Apart from what they did for a living, we
know very little about the early lives of any of these disciples. In the
same way, we actually know very little of what Jesus did in the first 30
years of his life. Apart from one story in Luke's gospel of Jesus as a boy,
we jump straight from his birth narratives to his baptism at around
30 years old. In between we have what is sometimes called his 'silent
years', 'lost years' or 'missing years'. There was a medieval legend that
Jesus was brought over to Britain as a boy, which is apparently the
inspiration behind William Blake's famous hymn 'Jerusalem': 'And
did those feet in ancient time walk upon England's mountains green?'
Jesus' missing years were probably far less glamorous – in all likeli-
hood, he was simply training as a carpenter in Galilee.

Once, on a day off, I decided to visit Barry, a town around 15 miles from
where I live in Cardiff. While there, I had some uplifting moments of
spiritual clarity and joy. I found the ruined chapel of St Baruc, a sixth-
century monk after whom the town is named. (When Cadoc arrived in

Wales with his disciple Baruc, he had forgotten a precious manuscript on Flat Holm Island in the Bristol Channel, so he sent Baruc back to collect it. Unfortunately, the boat capsized, and Baruc drowned. The chapel was thus built for him.) I spent some time of silence in these holy ruins, before I walked to the end of Friars Point peninsula, where I stood at the top of an iron age cairn and marvelled at the wonderful panoramic view of the Bristol Channel.

After these uplifting spiritual moments, I set off on the long trudge back to the car through the town's streets. To top it all, it began to rain. I started to accept that this ordinary, rather dull walk would dampen the inspiring memory of the sacred site and beautiful countryside. I then remembered the missing years of both Jesus and his disciples. It is easy to fall into the trap of thinking God is only in the important and breathtaking moments in our lives. So, as I walked, I challenged myself to see God in everything I saw. An unshaven young man walked past, pushing an empty pushchair and smoking a cigarette. I walked past a small school, where I could hear the laughter of children. I noticed an impressive school garden that had been immaculately tended by teachers and pupils. A woman, dressed all in white, came out of a shop clutching an enormous bottle of Coke and a small bottle of vodka. A friendly old lady came over and started chatting to me, and, as I looked back at her rough skin and dirty clothes, I saw God's light shine through her eyes. I continued walking past an empty playground, which had not seen a lick of paint for maybe 30 or 40 years. Then a beautifully dressed woman hurried past, walking her dog, looking so out of place as she avoided an old ironing board that had been discarded by the side of the road. As I got back to the car, I thanked God for allowing me to see his light despite the rain and mess. In fact, I thanked him for allowing me to see his light *in* the rain and mess. I thanked him for being there in the ordinariness of that journey back to the car.

It's relatively easy to see God in the special, uplifting moments in our lives, and we also find ourselves meeting him in the difficult and painful times. But God is to be found in the in-between times, too, in the missing years. 'Life, in its humdrum sense, is worth avoiding', bleakly asserts 80s rock star Morrissey in the biopic *England is Mine* (2017). As Christians, the challenge is not to avoid those times, but rather to open our eyes to discovering God in those ordinary moments. In the book *The Old Ways* (Penguin, 2012), Robert MacFarlane describes a walk that he had made a thousand times before, in the fields by his house. But this time he was walking at night, after it had been snowing all day. His eyes were opened anew to the beauty and the wonder of that pathway. He writes, 'The snow caused everything to exceed itself and the moonlight caused everything to double itself.'

Our lives have occasional highs and occasional lows, but, most of the time, they can be rather mundane. As Christians, we need to remember that God is present in the everyday, ordinary moments of our lives. Our God is also the God of the in-between times. He is the God of the humdrum, the monotonous and the commonplace. With him, those moments don't stay mundane. He brings joy, hope and beauty to even the most ordinary moments. He certainly dwells in the highs and lows, but he also lives in our missing years, and, when we actively recognise him in the tapestry of our everyday lives, he makes the ordinary extraordinary. God causes 'everything to exceed itself' and his light causes 'everything to double itself'.

Reflection

Meister Eckhart, the 14th-century theologian, wrote that 'we are all meant to be mothers of God, for God is always needing to be born'. In other words, our call is to look beyond the ordinary and to search for God in our midst, however he comes to us. Take some space and time to reflect on the past 24 hours. First, think of where God's light has shone in a clear and obvious way – perhaps through the beauty of nature or the kindness of family and friends. Now take time to think of the in-between times – where has his light shone in your more ordinary, mundane, everyday moments?

Sunday

Good news

Accept one another, then, just as Christ accepted you, in order to bring praise to God. For I tell you that Christ has become a servant of the Jews on behalf of God's truth, so that the promises made to the patriarchs might be confirmed and, moreover, that the Gentiles might glorify God for his mercy. As it is written:

> 'Therefore I will praise you among the Gentiles;
> I will sing the praises of your name.'

Again, it says,

> 'Rejoice, you Gentiles, with his people.'

And again,

> 'Praise the Lord, all you Gentiles;
> let all the peoples extol him.'

And again, Isaiah says,

> 'The Root of Jesse will spring up,
> one who will arise to rule over the nations;
> in him the Gentiles will hope.'

May the God of hope fill you with all joy and peace as you trust in him, so that you may overflow with hope by the power of the Holy Spirit.

ROMANS 15:7–13

When I was younger, I loved comedy sketch shows, like *Monty Python's Flying Circus*, *The Two Ronnies*, *Not the Nine O'Clock News* and *The Fast Show*. I still remember many of the catchphrases and punchlines, and I annoy my children by repeating them endlessly. One recurring sketch was of a French philosopher musing on the meaning of life. In the tradition of 20th-century French philosophy, he had a rather depressing outlook. In one episode, he sat, staring at half a glass of milk. Then, looking into the camera and in a gloomy French accent, he asserted, 'Some people look at half a glass of milk and say that it is half empty; other people look at half a glass of milk and say that it is half full. I look at half a glass of milk and say that it is sour.' In today's passage we are led to ask how we view our faith. Are we glass-half-full or glass-half-empty Christians? Are we the people of hope and optimism or of fear and cynicism?

The film critic Mark Kermode points out that the most memorable film reviews are not those that are glowing and positive, but the ones that are acerbic, biting and critical. He lists dozens of these reviews – from the review of *The Flintstones* that simply said, 'Yabbadabba-don't', to the review of *Vampires Suck* that stated, 'Vampires Suck, but this film sucks more!' Nothing sells better than bad news, he concludes, as he inverts a popular saying: 'Good news is no news.'

Increasingly, 'good news is no news' is also true of society at large. We have an inclination towards cynicism, distrust and scepticism, and we often revel in bad news. Our news channels are not full of uplifting events that happen daily in our communities but rather of disasters and crime. Our tendency towards revelling in pessimism and negativity seems to have developed hand-in-hand with a loss of hope in our society, exacerbated in recent years by political upheaval and a ruthless pandemic. Hopelessness, despair and malaise are some of the most damaging elements that we face today – in our society, politics and faith.

Yet Jesus inspires us to open our eyes to the good news and hope that still exist all around. Many of the hymns that we sing in churches come from a time when life was so much more taxing than our lives today. Still, these hymns continue to hold on to a message of joy and expectation. The slaves who wrote and sang the African-American spirituals, despite the terrible hardships they faced, never lost that sense of hope in their songs. Similarly, many of the celebrated reformers of the past century have been rooted in Christian hope, and their struggle never led them to cynicism or hopelessness. The great civil rights campaigners, for example, were inspired by dreams of future equality, rather than being shackled by nightmares of their present situation. 'Hope is being able to see that there is light despite all of the darkness,' wrote Archbishop Desmond Tutu.

In our church nativity one year, my eldest son was given the job of holding placards with the words 'good news' and 'bad news' on them. The congregation were encouraged to shout 'Pass it on, pass it on' when he showed the 'good news' placard and 'Oh dear, oh dear' when he showed the other placard. Unfortunately, he got a bit confused and ended up lifting the wrong placards at the wrong times. So, the congregation ended up shouting 'Pass it on, pass it on' when bad news was given and shouting 'Oh dear, oh dear' when good news was announced!

Too often we fall into that very trap, as we pass on any bad news that we hear and become cynical at the good news. We need to step off that treadmill of pessimism and show that we are people of new life, hope and resurrection. Even our word 'gospel', which comes from the Old English words *god*, meaning 'good', and *spel*, meaning 'news', makes it clear that we are a faith of good news, inspiration and transformation. We don't need to see things as half empty or half full. Rather, we are called simply to open our eyes to the promise and hope all around us.

Reflection

The most potent threats to both our society and our churches are hopelessness and cynicism. Once they catch hold, they spread like infections and isolate us from light and life, as we concentrate on weaknesses we perceive in ourselves, in our churches or in the wider society. Today, open your eyes to the good news all around you, whether on the TV news, in newspapers or in the lives of family or friends. Commit yourself to being a person of hope.

Monday

JOY – Just Open Your eyes

This is what the Lord says:

'Sing with joy for Jacob;
    shout for the foremost of the nations.
Make your praises heard, and say,
    "Lord, save your people,
    the remnant of Israel."
See, I will bring them from the land of the north
    and gather them from the ends of the earth.
Among them will be the blind and the lame,
    expectant mothers and women in labour;
    a great throng will return.
They will come with weeping;
    they will pray as I bring them back.
I will lead them beside streams of water
    on a level path where they will not stumble,
because I am Israel's father,
    and Ephraim is my firstborn son.
'Hear the word of the Lord, you nations;
    proclaim it in distant coastlands:
"He who scattered Israel will gather them
    and will watch over his flock like a shepherd."
For the Lord will deliver Jacob
    and redeem them from the hand of those stronger than they.
They will come and shout for joy on the heights of Zion;
    they will rejoice in the bounty of the Lord –
the grain, the new wine and the olive oil,
    the young of the flocks and herds.
They will be like a well-watered garden,
    and they will sorrow no more.

> Then young women will dance and be glad,
>   young men and old as well.
> I will turn their mourning into gladness;
>   I will give them comfort and joy instead of sorrow.'

JEREMIAH 31:7–13

Recently, we had a family day out on a cold, windy and rainy day in the mountains of the Brecon Beacons. After getting out of the car, we realised that our eldest son was wearing his trainers rather than his walking boots. As we'd come that far, we decided to plough on with our walk. Unfortunately, the footpath was flooded in parts, and it was becoming a difficult and miserable walk. As we struggled to traverse our way, there was a sudden scream. I looked round to see my son flying through the air. He had slipped, and his landing took him straight into a muddy puddle. Initially, we were worried about his fall, but then we saw he had started laughing and we all started laughing as well. From then on, the walk was great fun as he started to amuse us by purposefully slipping into any muddy water he could find.

The religious concept of *hwyl* is something that is distinctive in my country's history. It is a Welsh word that originally referred to a sense of fun and joy in our worship. The great Welsh revivals were rooted in religious fervour, zeal and joy. That same Welsh word *hwyl* is now in everyday usage to simply mean 'fun' or, when used as a departing remark, 'have fun'. 'Fun' is exactly what those 18th- and 19th-century Welsh Christians had in their chapels. Church historians describe whole congregations singing, laughing and dancing as they worshipped.

Today's passage is from the prophet Jeremiah. He wrote these words at a time of pain and misery for his country and his people, in the years leading up to the fall of Jerusalem to the Babylonians in 587BC. Jeremiah himself is even sometimes referred to as 'the weeping prophet'. Yet our passage today paints a vivid, joyful picture of happiness, fun and dancing.

Sometimes life is so difficult and painful that humour is certainly not appropriate. Most of the time, though, joyfulness and laughter are not far away from us, even when we are struggling. I once led an all-age service at a church in which I encouraged children to consider that the letters J, O and Y can stand for Just Open Your eyes. The children seemed to embrace this idea and, with many hands shooting up, were eager to tell me of all the joy they had experienced in recent days. In reality, though, we sometimes go through our lives as if our eyes were wide shut. We don't notice all the wonderful things around us which could bring joy. The rain, mud and cold were making us miserable on that walk in the Brecon Beacons, but then we saw my eldest son fall and laugh, and it changed everything. It gave us a sense of perspective and grounded us in one of life's many paradoxes – laughter can break through at the most surprising times. We opened our eyes and found JOY!

It was, to me, no surprise that the children in that all-age service really took to that idea of JOY. Children seem to live every moment to the full, whether they are babies smiling at shadows on the wall or school children laughing and joking in the yard. Perhaps this is something of what Jesus meant when he encouraged his disciples to become like children to experience the kingdom of God (Matthew 18:3). If we can capture some of the infectious joy of children in our own lives, then the Welsh *hwyl* of the revivalists will be present in our hearts. After all, when we embrace joy and laughter, we are treading on sacred ground.

Reflection

A few years back, a BBC radio programme asked listeners to send in any sounds that cheered them up. All sorts of sounds were submitted, including the sizzle of sausages frying, the crunch of leaves being walked on, the rustle of trees in the wind, the crash of waves against the shore, the laughter of children in a playground, the purr of a cat seeking attention and the pop of a cork from a bottle of champagne! In the next day, try to pause when something makes you smile or brings some joy in your life. For now, though, take some time to consider the past day – what made you smile or laugh? Thank God for moments of joy, those times of hwyl, whatever the outward circumstances of our lives.

Tuesday

Active waiting

Out of the depths I cry to you, Lord;
   Lord, hear my voice.
Let your ears be attentive
   to my cry for mercy.
If you, Lord, kept a record of sins,
   Lord, who could stand?
But with you there is forgiveness,
   so that we can, with reverence, serve you.
I wait for the Lord, my whole being waits,
   and in his word I put my hope.
I wait for the Lord
   more than watchmen wait for the morning,
   more than watchmen wait for the morning.

PSALM 130:1–6

Lent is a season of waiting for that future expectation – the resurrection. Most of us don't enjoy having to wait for things. When my youngest son was four, we explained to him about the season of Lent and then regretted it for the next 40 days! He just couldn't cope with the wait and so we had many tears and tantrums as he processed each day's answer to 'How many sleeps till Easter eggs, Daddy?'

Perhaps the word 'wait' is not so different from its homophone, 'weight'. There can be a heaviness about waiting. There's a story of a teacher picking up his glass of water and asking his students how heavy it was. All sorts of answers were called out, ranging from 5 ounces to 30 ounces. The teacher then informed them that the absolute weight had no bearing on his own experience of the weight. 'The weight depends on how long I hold it,' he concluded. 'If I hold it for a minute, it's no problem at all. If I hold it for an hour, I'll have a slight ache in my arm. If I hold it for a day, then my whole arm will start to feel numb and paralysed. In each case, the weight of the glass doesn't change, but the longer I hold it, the heavier it becomes.'

Sometimes, when we are waiting for something or someone, it can be rather frustrating and wearisome, like an ache in the arm. It can, for example, be a somewhat unpleasant experience when we are waiting in a queue in a supermarket or we're waiting for a friend who's late once again. But waiting can also be far more serious and severe. Ultimately, waiting can weigh us down. It can be like carrying a heavy load for a long period. It can numb us and paralyse us when we are waiting for recovery from illness, for depression to lift, for light to break through grief, for test results or for the hurt of broken relationships to heal.

Nothing can completely take away the darkness of this difficult waiting. But in all our waiting, our faith can make a difference. Jesus can make both the darkness and the heavy load lighter. In this sense, waiting doesn't have to always be so frustrating or painful. After all, there are two seasons of waiting in the church calendar – Advent and Lent – and both have something in common. Both end in new life and joy. Interestingly, almost all the verses in the Bible that mention 'waiting' do not relate it to heaviness, pain and oppression. Instead, they challenge us to view our waiting in a different way – relating waiting to hope. Perhaps this could be called 'active waiting', as our waiting helps us to truly find the kingdom in our everyday lives.

Not that this 'active waiting' will necessarily come naturally to us. Sometimes our waiting is looking forward in anticipation of a good event. This can lead us to live our lives in the future, rather than enjoy the gift of waiting. It once dawned on me that I had spent so much time thinking how I was looking forward to the next stage of my children's development – to when they learnt to crawl, then when they walked, then when they talked, then when they would actually enjoy watching football with me. I was looking at photos of them recently and realised how much I had missed of their development by looking to the future.

I now challenge myself to appreciate where they are now – you could call it 'resting in the waiting for the next stage' – rather than wishing the next stage would come quickly.

There are other times, though, when our waiting is not to do with anticipation, but rather we are forced to wait due to illness or a traumatic event. The lockdowns that resulted from the Covid-19 pandemic, for example, put all our lives on hold. While such waiting can be painful and difficult, we can still wait actively when we face adversity. During an intense period of pain after a back injury, I had to wait for almost twelve months for an operation. As a result, for that time I was laid up in bed for most of each day. I would venture out for very short daily strolls, and I taught myself to truly appreciate those walks – the beauty of nature, the conversation of friends who accompanied me, the silence when I walked alone or the uplifting music when I took my iPod. This was all God at work, and, in spite of my continuing pain, I could not help but celebrate his wonderful, mysterious and holy gift of life.

Reflection

The poet Ralph Waldo Emerson asked, 'How much of human life is lost in waiting?' Reflect on that quotation, how much of our lives are wasted as we wait for the future to happen? Active waiting is about opening our eyes to God's light in our journeys, however long and difficult the wait, however heavy and burdensome the weight. Next time you have to wait for something, commit yourself to actively waiting in whatever way helps you to connect with God.

Wednesday

Walking and creation

How many are your works, Lord!
   In wisdom you made them all;
   the earth is full of your creatures.
There is the sea, vast and spacious,
   teeming with creatures beyond number –
   living things both large and small.
There the ships go to and fro,
   and Leviathan, which you formed to frolic there.
All creatures look to you
   to give them their food at the proper time.
When you give it to them,
   they gather it up;
when you open your hand,
   they are satisfied with good things.
When you hide your face,
   they are terrified;
when you take away their breath,
   they die and return to the dust.
When you send your Spirit,
   they are created,
   and you renew the face of the ground.
May the glory of the Lord endure for ever;
   may the Lord rejoice in his works –
he who looks at the earth, and it trembles,
   who touches the mountains, and they smoke.
I will sing to the Lord all my life;
   I will sing praise to my God as long as I live.

PSALM 104:24–33

I was raised in north Wales and, from a young age, I was fascinated by stories of the medieval pilgrims who would walk from Basingwerk Abbey, near Holywell in the north-east of Wales, to the furthest western tip of the Llŷn Peninsula. There, they would board a boat to the mystical Ynys Enlli (Bardsey Island). The island is said to be the graveyard of 20,000 Celtic saints and was so important in the Middle Ages that it was known as 'the Rome of Britain'. Up until recently, I had never set foot on this beautiful, remote and tranquil island. A few years back, though, I took up the challenge of walking that pilgrimage route, which is around 140 miles. It was to be an uplifting and life-affirming journey, but also hugely challenging and difficult.

My memories of the journey I undertook can now be very simply broken down into, first, my pain and, second, God's presence. I had not certainly expected the walk to be as difficult as it was. Despite my long-standing back condition, I had built up strength to be able to walk long distances. However, I had not factored in how easy it was to get lost (which led to many extra miles of walking), how uneven the terrain was (I should have known that Snowdonia is quite hilly), how changeable the weather was (again, I should have guessed that) and how many obstacles I'd have to overcome (not least electric fences, barbed wire, gnashing farm dogs and wading through so much thick mud). On top of this, tendinitis in my knee and a recurrence of my back injury made the walk a huge challenge.

Although the walk was fraught with difficulties, it was also blessed with countless moments of joy and beauty, where God's presence broke through. These moments sparked what John Henry Newman called the 'illative sense' – the sense that allows everyday moments to connect us with the divine. In the Old Testament psalms and elsewhere in scripture, writers bask in the glory of creation. As in our passage today, both land and sea are seen as marvels of God's created order. In fact, the psalmist even includes ships – that is, vessels made by humans – in his description of the wonders of the world. In other words, *everything* is God's and, when we connect with him through the world around us, we cannot fail to be uplifted and inspired.

On my long walk, I felt palpably close to God as I walked in the foot-steps of countless other pilgrims – I experienced the wonder of the creation story as I gazed on the most spectacular scenery; I saw the burning bush in seemingly ordinary trees that I walked past; I tasted the bread of heaven in the much-needed meals I devoured; and I met Jesus himself in those who joined me for sections of the walk and in strangers I met on the way. I felt as if I was witnessing God's kingdom breaking through each day and, like the psalmist, I was led through wonder to worship. I was, in the beautiful words of the late bishop Saunders Davies, 'experiencing creation at its most translucent', glimpsing the grandeur and glory of its creator. As such, pilgrimages realign our priorities and, when we return home, we have been trans-formed and our eyes are opened anew to encountering God in our journeys.

Walks, of course, need not be long and arduous to lead to such moving encounters. In the famous Welsh poem 'Y Llwynog' ('The fox'), R. Williams Parry describes coming face-to-face with a fox on a beautiful Sunday in July. The bells of the church are ringing, calling him to go to church, but he chooses to walk up the mountain instead. As he's walking a fox steps out in front of him. This surprise appearance stuns him into silence and stillness. To him, this was as much a spiritual event as when he attends church. The moment doesn't last long, as the fox soon scuttles away, but he compares that fleeting moment of joy to seeing a shooting star – it lifts your heart and then it's gone.

Walking as a hobby is often referred to as hiking or rambling. On my pilgrimage, though, I embraced the word 'sauntering' to refer to my journey. Not that I was taking my time or walking slowly, as the word might imply these days. Rather, I had been inspired by the etymology of that word given by the poet Henry David Thoreau in his famous essay on 'Walking'. In the Middle Ages, he wrote, wanderers would be asked where they were going by people in the villages through which they were passing. To pass themselves off as pilgrims, they would reply, '*A la sainte terre*' – 'to the Holy Land'. They therefore became known as 'sainte-terre-ers', and thus the word 'saunterer' was born. There is something beautiful about the idea that our walking is related to holiness and to our faith. Whether we are rambling long distances in the countryside, wandering around our local park or simply walking in the streets around our homes, we can commit ourselves to saunter through them – opening our eyes to the Holy Land, to God's presence, all around us.

Reflection

Whatever the weather today, go out for a short walk. Try to saunter on your walk – notice the holiness of God's creation, open your eyes to his presence on your walk and, like the psalmist, praise him for the marvels of his creation.

Thursday

Stumbling blocks

Rejoice in the Lord always. I will say it again: rejoice! Let your gentleness be evident to all. The Lord is near. Do not be anxious about anything, but in every situation, by prayer and petition, with thanksgiving, present your requests to God. And the peace of God, which transcends all understanding, will guard your hearts and your minds in Christ Jesus.

Finally, brothers and sisters, whatever is true, whatever is noble, whatever is right, whatever is pure, whatever is lovely, whatever is admirable – if anything is excellent or praiseworthy – think about such things. Whatever you have learned or received or heard from me, or seen in me – put it into practice. And the God of peace will be with you.

PHILIPPIANS 4:4–9

One morning, during a recent retreat in Pembrokeshire, I decided to go for a walk on the coastal path. It was all going well – for about five minutes. At that point, though, I looked down and realised how high the cliffs were. Suddenly, I was terrified and froze on the spot. Quite quickly, I started sweating and shaking with fear. After standing in the same place for around a quarter of an hour, I realised the only way that I could get back to the retreat centre was getting down on all fours, focusing only on the dusty path in front of me and crawling back the way I came. You can just imagine the looks I got from people walking past me! It was only when I got safely back to my room and I was relaxing on my sofa that I looked at some of the photographs that I'd taken in the few minutes before the fear kicked in. The photos were stunning – the scenery was so beautiful – but I'd separated myself from it all because I was crawling around like a dog.

This is true of life in general. When we are scared, when we are fearful, we fail to see the beauty and wonder all around us. At the beginning of the recent pandemic, for example, many of us found ourselves caught up in fear as the world went into lockdown. As a born worrier, I was certainly not immune to this anxiety. Being released from the grip of this fear came, for me, through spiritual means. The 'incarnation'– God coming to us in Jesus – allows us to go beyond fear or anxiety and to see the world differently. Jesus came to see the world through our eyes, so we can see the world through his. Through him, we are able to recognise the beauty in the ordinary, the wonder in the everyday. In this sense, the 'incarnation' allows us to witness Christ in everything – even in the lowliest person or the most mundane event. That's the real challenge of being people of faith – to open our eyes to God's presence in our lives, whether in the love of friends and family, the wonder of the countryside, the warmth of a smile, uplifting music or art, or a kind word or gesture.

But when we fear things, we fail to see their ultimate worth or their beauty. And it's not merely fear that can become a stumbling block to us recognising Jesus in others. Many other things can get in the way – stress, prejudice and anxiety, to name but a few. The Oscar-nominated film *Wonder* (2017), based on a 2012 R.J. Palacio novel of the same name, is the story of a 10-year-old boy with Treacher Collins syndrome who moves to a new school. Auggie's condition means he has a facial deformity, following 27 different invasive surgeries. It is only when his new schoolmates get to know him and move beyond their prejudice against his appearance, that they recognise what a 'wonder' he is and start to open their eyes to the beauty behind his scars. As his head teacher tells the parents of a pupil who had been bullying him, 'Auggie can't change the way he looks, so maybe we can change the way we see.'

Opening our eyes to God's presence means noticing and naming our fears and anxieties and then pushing ourselves beyond them to an awareness and appreciation of his world. Our personal stumbling blocks can stop us truly living in the present moment and so stop us being alive in its fullest sense. By facing them, we allow beauty and wonder to be birthed in our lives as we recognise the Christ in all. After all, as the third-century theologian Irenaeus wrote, 'The glory of God is a person fully alive.'

Reflection

Think of a time in your life when something made you anxious or fearful, perhaps as the result of the pandemic, or, indeed, another time entirely. How did you get through this time? Ask God for help with those times when you still feel anxious or worried. Now commit yourself to going beyond any fear or anxiety you might feel in the coming weeks and to looking for Jesus' presence in the things you do and the places you go.

Friday

Colours of day

When he was at the table with them, he took bread, gave thanks, broke it and began to give it to them. Then their eyes were opened and they recognised him, and he disappeared from their sight. They asked each other, 'Were not our hearts burning within us while he talked with us on the road and opened the Scriptures to us?'

They got up and returned at once to Jerusalem. There they found the Eleven and those with them, assembled together and saying, 'It is true! The Lord has risen and has appeared to Simon.' Then the two told what had happened on the way, and how Jesus was recognised by them when he broke the bread.

LUKE 24:30–35

When I was chaplain at Cardiff University I got a call from a concerned mother at 6.30 am. She was upset that her son had begun to hold extreme views – and I was upset to be woken up so early! In my early morning haze, I tried to reassure her that youthful zeal was behind this young man's dualistic view of life. 'Students often see things as black-and-white,' I said to her, 'and they don't realise life is mostly shades of grey.' I will never forget her reply. 'No, Revd Hughes,' she said. 'You've got that wrong. Life isn't shades of grey; not at all. Life is red and blue and orange and brown and yellow and green and purple.'

In today's passage we are thrown forward to the resurrection, when Jesus appears to two of his followers, who are walking to a place called Emmaus. One peculiarity of this account is that these disciples are going the wrong way. The whole trajectory of Luke's gospel is pointing towards one place – Jerusalem. Suddenly we are faced with two disciples, disheartened and grieving, walking away from Jerusalem. Furthermore, some scholars think that Emmaus, where they were walking towards, may well have been a Roman garrison town; in other words it was a town that had an enemy military base in it. The disciples were going the wrong way, they were taking the wrong path.

Then we have the second strange fact about this story, to which our passage alludes. When Jesus appears and walks with them, they don't even recognise him. In some of the old films about Jesus that I used to be forced to watch in R.E. lessons, this would be explained by showing the setting sun getting in the eyes of the weary disciples. But that get-out clause is not particularly plausible. After all, it's not that these disciples don't recognise him for a moment or two – Jesus walks with them and talks to them for a *long* time. Also, we have to remember that this is not the only account of resurrection where the risen Christ is not recognised – Mary thought Jesus was the gardener and the disciples who were fishing didn't recognise their master.

So, these heavy-hearted followers of Jesus were walking the wrong way and they didn't recognise their master even when he was travelling with them. Throughout the journey, Jesus had been explaining the scriptures to them. They were so taken with this teaching that they persuaded him to stay. But it was not until today's passage, when he broke bread, that they realised who he was. In other words, they recognised him in a reminder of the love that he'd shown in the last supper and on the cross. At such a dark time in their lives, the colour returned to them. And that inspires them to walk the path immediately back to Jerusalem the next morning. Interestingly, the disciples on the road to Emmaus never even got there. Once they truly recognised Jesus was with them, they turned their lives around, quite literally, and went back with joy in their hearts.

Similar to these disciples, all of us are often walking the wrong way, doing our own things, stuck in our own self-centred ways of being. God allows that – he gives us free will and doesn't force us to walk his way. Yet, whichever path we are taking, Jesus is walking with us, accompanying us on our ups and downs, standing with us in both our joys and our difficulties and coming to us in the colour of our everyday lives.

Like the disciples on their journey, though, we don't always recognise him. We may, like them, grasp hints of Jesus in teachings about him – in beliefs, theology, discussion and the creed. But it is only when we witness his love that we open our eyes fully to Jesus' presence. Just as the disciples recognised Jesus in the breaking of the bread, an act that symbolised his sacrifice of love, we will discover him in our concrete experiences of love – in our fellowship with one another, in our local communities, in our everyday relationships, in the wonder of the countryside around us, in the beauty of art and music, in the joy of laughter and in the small acts of kindness we witness each day.

So, God opens our eyes to see beyond black and white. He allows us to recognise life for what it really is – full of colour, vitality and beauty – even in difficult and painful times. He does not want us to box him in with black-and-white thinking, nor does he want us to dilute his message to shades of grey. Rather, he wants us to recognise him daily in the red, blue, orange, brown, yellow, green and purple and in all the other beautiful colours that we are blessed to experience in our lives.

Reflection

A prayer to be prayed slowly and mindfully – allow each word and phrase to inspire your walk with God:

> *Lord of creation,*
> *open our eyes to the wonderful colour in our lives,*
> *help us to recognise Jesus' grace, forgiveness, joy and hope,*
> *   whatever the outward circumstances of our journeys.*
> *As we spend time in silence, reassure us that you are walking*
> *   alongside us, bringing us moments of blessing, both in times of*
> *   difficulty and times of joy.*
> *In Jesus' name,*
> *Amen*

Saturday

Attitude of gratitude

Now on his way to Jerusalem, Jesus travelled along the border between Samaria and Galilee. As he was going into a village, ten men who had leprosy met him. They stood at a distance and called out in a loud voice, 'Jesus, Master, have pity on us!'
 When he saw them, he said, 'Go, show yourselves to the priests.' And as they went, they were cleansed.
 One of them, when he saw he was healed, came back, praising God in a loud voice. He threw himself at Jesus' feet and thanked him – and he was a Samaritan.
 Jesus asked, 'Were not all ten cleansed? Where are the other nine? Has no one returned to give praise to God except this foreigner?' Then he said to him, 'Rise and go; your faith has made you well.'

LUKE 17:11–19

On the morning of the 2016 EU referendum, I took a class assembly for a group of 12-year-olds. I thought I'd ease them into a discussion about Brexit by asking them to list countries in the European Union. A hand shot up. A young lad said, 'Sir, is Brazil in the EU?' A girl's hand then went up, and she asked, 'What about Nigeria, sir?' That assembly was not exactly a roaring success. I was, therefore, dreading my next assembly. When that day came, I asked them what they were grateful for in their lives. After my previous experience, I was expecting them to struggle to list three or four things, and then we'd move on. I was amazed. For over 20 minutes I was scribbling their answers on the board – their family, friends, a free country, a safe country, animals, countryside, sport, their talents, a roof over their heads, education – and the list went on. They even included the elderly, adding, 'like you, sir'. Those young people may not know geography, but, boy, did they know gratitude!

In our passage today, Jesus heals ten lepers. Those lepers then had to go, as was the custom in Jewish law, to the local priests to be officially designated as clean. Only one, a Samaritan, went back to thank Jesus. Where were the other nine?

Biblical scholars posit two possibilities. First, they may have been too scared to go back. Jesus was a marked man, hated by the authorities they'd just reported to. They may have felt that it was too difficult and dangerous to go back to Jesus. Second, they may have felt they had no time to go back. They'd probably been ill for years, and so it is likely there was only one place they wanted to be – out partying and celebrating with their family and friends. After all, they would have been separated from them since they became ill. So, it seems it was either difficulty or lack of time that meant they didn't go back to thank the person who had transformed their lives.

When our youngest child was a toddler, we spent many months rehearsing his pleases and thank yous. At night we would encourage him to reflect on the past day and say 'Thank you' to God in prayer. He'd lie down with his hands clasped together and list people and things he appreciated. Children seem to instinctively want to thank someone for the good things in their lives. Both the group of 12-year-olds at the class assembly and my son's evening prayers really taught me something about gratitude – they made me stop and ask myself how often we, as adults, express gratitude for the good things in our lives.

When we don't, it can be for the same reasons that the nine lepers didn't go back to Jesus. First, it sometimes seems too difficult for us to be truly thankful. Perhaps we have unhappiness in our lives – depression, illness, disability, grief – and so it's difficult for us to look at the gifts in our lives and give thanks. Nothing is more frustrating and annoying than when something bad happens in our lives and someone says, 'Yes, but look at the good things that you still have – count your blessings.' No one should minimise unhappiness, pain, grief and suffering. But we Christians are also people of hope and resurrection.

So we need to be courageous, as the Samaritan leper was, and we need to face, and give thanks for, the moments of light we have in our lives, however they come to us.

Second, sometimes we're simply too busy to give thanks. One of the astronauts who had walked on the moon was asked in an interview if he had any regrets in life. He explained that, when he stepped on to the surface of the moon, he looked back at earth and just stood still, in wonder and in awe of its beauty. Then he suddenly thought, 'Oh, I'm meant to be collecting rocks' and went on with his work. He explained that he regretted not taking another few moments to appreciate the view. How often are we all too busy 'collecting rocks' to take time out to appreciate our lives, to thank God for the blessings in our lives?

Sometimes in the pain or the busyness of life, gratitude is difficult. We need to make sure we have both courage and time, so we can open our eyes to God's light in our life and thank him for what he has given us. As Psalm 106:1 puts it, 'Praise the Lord. Give thanks to the Lord, for he is good; his love endures forever.'

Reflection

In a moment of silence, think about what you have in your life for which you want to give thanks. Challenge yourself to be that one leper who went back and not the nine who found it either too difficult or too time-consuming.

═══ **WEEK 2** ═══

Open our ears to your call

Sunday

Vocation

The word of the Lord came to me, saying,

'Before I formed you in the womb I knew you,
before you were born I set you apart;
I appointed you as a prophet to the nations.'

'Alas, Sovereign Lord,' I said, 'I do not know how to speak;
I am too young.'
But the Lord said to me, 'Do not say, "I am too young." You
must go to everyone I send you to and say whatever I command you. Do not be afraid of them, for I am with you and will
rescue you,' declares the Lord.
Then the Lord reached out his hand and touched my mouth
and said to me, 'I have put my words in your mouth. See, today
I appoint you over nations and kingdoms to uproot and tear
down, to destroy and overthrow, to build and to plant.'

JEREMIAH 1:4–10

For more than five years, I was the director of vocations for an Anglican
diocese in Wales. I would often visit congregations to explore what
a vocation entails. To many it brings to mind a person who gives up
everything to follow a worthy cause. But the root of the word is the
Latin *vocarere*, which simply means 'to call'. God, of course, does not
only call people who are fantastically talented or terribly worthy. God
calls each and every one of us, whoever we are, whatever our background. He calls us to help him in his work of bringing love, hope and
peace to our situations. In today's passage, Jeremiah is only a child.
God, though, reassures him that he's not too young – just as we ourselves are never too anything to be 'called' by God, whatever our age
or background.

When we are thinking about our lives and to what we should commit our time, talents and resources, we might automatically consider what would be good for us and what our own priorities are. However, God's calling challenges us not merely to ask what *we* want from life, but what life is demanding of us. Each one of us has been given gifts from God. Some of these are innate talents, abilities and personality traits, while others we may have worked hard to hone. Either way, we owe it to God to use those gifts wisely.

Singing is, sadly, *not* one of my talents. Still, I have a secret passion to which I rarely admit – I love karaoke! In fact, I have sung in karaoke bars across the globe – from Berlin to Brisbane. My signature song, which I save until the end of the night, after I have already massacred 'Daydream Believer', 'Mack the Knife' and 'Hey Jude', is Frank Sinatra's 'My Way'. Each time I croon that hit, though, I always feel rather uncomfortable with the lyrics, which seem to sum up modern life's individualistic attitude. The song criticises 'the one who kneels' and praises those who listen to no one but themselves. As Christians, however, the process should be reversed – we need to be the ones who kneel and the ones who are listening, not to our own desires but for God's call. God is asking us to consider how we are being called to use our talents and personalities to contribute positively to the circumstances we are facing. How can we use our gifts to bring just a little light to the world around us? What does the environment in which we find ourselves need in order to be made whole? Where do we fit in?

Vocation, of course, is a journey that takes each of us on different paths. My own moment of clarity came while sitting in a small chapel in Carmarthen in west Wales. I was a full-time university academic at the time. As I sat in that chapel, I looked up and saw the words 'feed my sheep' in a stained-glass window. For a moment, I thought I was being called to follow my grandfather into farming! Then it dawned on me that these words were the ones which Jesus spoke to the disciple Peter. Like the disciples 2,000 years ago, I felt the words were being spoken directly to me, challenging me to stand alongside people in their joys and sorrows, encouraging them and offering them God's peace and comfort. This episode led me to give up my lectureship and offer myself for training for ordination. Other people's callings, of course, take them in all sorts of different directions – to teach, to work as nurses or doctors, to serve in a shop, to run a business, to be mothers, fathers or grandparents, to be musicians or artists or to take roles in churches, such as churchwardens or choir members.

And, of course, we can be called, again and again, to different tasks and roles. When our youngest son was two years old, he discovered the wonder of lollipops, and, as a result, we discovered that sticking a lolly in his mouth would keep our very lively little Kojak quiet for a long time. Being called by God is sometimes like a lollipop – a once-and-for-all experience that can last a long time. My daughter's favourite sweets, on the other hand, are Starburst (or, for those of us over 40, Opal Fruits), which disappear much more quickly. Sometimes being called by God is more like enjoying a pack of those – we eat one, then another and another, and occasionally we put more than one in our mouths at the same time. We are, after all, given opportunities to follow God's call at many different points in our lives. Some of our vocations are lifelong, others last a season and then we move on to another calling, and sometimes we are living out different vocations at the same time. Through all this, one thing is certain – the question is never whether God is calling us, but whether we are listening.

Reflection

What is God calling you to now? What is God asking of you? It may be to something that your church needs you to do or it might be something outside of the church that your community desperately needs. Open your ears and listen to God's call on your life. The holocaust survivor Viktor Frankl wrote: 'It does not really matter what we expect from life, but rather what life expects from us.' What does life, what does God, expect of you?

Monday

Silence and God's call

That evening after sunset the people brought to Jesus all who were ill and demon-possessed. The whole town gathered at the door, and Jesus healed many who had various diseases. He also drove out many demons, but he would not let the demons speak because they knew who he was.

Very early in the morning, while it was still dark, Jesus got up, left the house and went off to a solitary place, where he prayed. Simon and his companions went to look for him, and when they found him, they exclaimed: 'Everyone is looking for you!'

MARK 1:32–37

Jesus' words in the New Testament are a great gift to us – they speak to us, teach us, challenge us and uplift us. We are, however, not merely called to listen to his words, but also to live his life. Again and again in the gospels we are told, almost in passing, that Jesus withdrew to be alone and to be with God. His times of reflection, prayer and silence can teach us as much as the words and actions that they bookend.

In a song entitled 'God's Blog', Jim Bob, former frontman of the 90s rock band Carter USM, describes God's deep sadness at witnessing the terrible way that people are treating each other. God is tempted to just delete everybody, but then he glances down and sees the first steps of a child, a beautiful sunset, a random act of kindness and, borrowing a phrase from French composer Claude Debussy, 'the space between the notes'. That phrase is intriguing. There is something quite beautiful about the idea. Most of us connect with uplifting melodies, but what we don't necessarily realise is that the silence between the notes is just as important as the notes themselves. If a piano were played without any spaces between the notes, we would not have music; it would be simply noise. This, of course, is the same for our lives. Communication, discussion and speaking out against injustice and hatred are all part of our call as Christians, but we also need times of silence, reflection and prayer. We need space between the notes. Otherwise, we end up with just noise.

Silence, though, is all too often neglected in the contemporary world. We talk, quite rightly, about the importance of being heard, having a voice and speaking our mind. But silence and reflection are rarely championed. My dad would often quote an old Welsh saying to me as a child: '*Tawed y doeth, annoeth ni thaw*' – 'Let the wise be silent, for the foolish will not.' In today's world, our lifestyles make silence difficult. Social media contributes to the noise in our lives, as we feel we have to tell the world our innermost thoughts or we constantly check on what others are posting.

The beauty of stillness and silence is too often underappreciated. Embracing the space between the notes allows us to step outside the hustle and bustle of this world and recharge our batteries. More than that, doing so opens ourselves to God's voice in our lives – to that 'still, small voice of calm', as the hymn 'Dear Lord and Father' puts it. After all, in the Old Testament, Elijah did not find God in the great and powerful wind, nor in the earthquake, nor the fire. God was found in the gentle whisper, the 'still, small voice of calm'.

When we take time in silence, to listen for God's voice, then we start to be transformed by his call. Desmond Tutu describes connecting with God in silence as similar to sitting next to a fire on a cold day. We don't have to *do* anything. We just feel the warmth and we somehow *take on* the attributes of the fire. The fire is warm, so we become warm. Likewise, we don't need to do anything when we take time for silence with God. We just need to feel his presence, and somehow we take on the attributes of God. God is love, so we become more like God – less judgemental and more loving. Then, when we leave that silence to speak and act, we speak and act out of wisdom, peace and love.

Reflection

Very simply, just take some time out today – to be still, to be silent, to be with God, to listen to him. Take time to experience and explore the space between the notes. Ask God in this silence to begin to transform you into his image – ask that, by sitting in his presence, you take on his attributes and become more loving and compassionate.

Tuesday

Our call to see Jesus in others

"Why have we fasted," they say,
    "and you have not seen it?
Why have we humbled ourselves,
    and you have not noticed?"
'Yet on the day of your fasting, you do as you please
    and exploit all your workers.
Your fasting ends in quarrelling and strife,
    and in striking each other with wicked fists.
You cannot fast as you do today
    and expect your voice to be heard on high.
Is this the kind of fast I have chosen,
    only a day for people to humble themselves?
Is it only for bowing one's head like a reed
    and for lying in sackcloth and ashes?
Is that what you call a fast,
    a day acceptable to the Lord?
'Is not this the kind of fasting I have chosen:
to loose the chains of injustice
    and untie the cords of the yoke,
to set the oppressed free
    and break every yoke?
Is it not to share your food with the hungry
    and to provide the poor wanderer with shelter –
when you see the naked, to clothe them,
    and not to turn away from your own flesh and blood?
Then your light will break forth like the dawn,
    and your healing will quickly appear;
then your righteousness will go before you,
    and the glory of the Lord will be your rear guard.

ISAIAH 58:3–8

On the day we moved into our vicarage, I was sitting in the living room with a fellow vicar, under the glow of a wonderful new lampshade. As we were chatting, my daughter came back from school and burst into the room. She looked straight up at the lampshade and stood staring at it in appreciation. I reminded her that she should have first greeted us when she walked into the room. 'Don't just look up,' I said, 'look across as well.' Quick as a flash, my colleague said, 'Well, there's your sermon for next week!' We both laughed and got on with our meeting, but those words stayed with me – 'Don't just look up; look across as well.'

In today's passage from Isaiah, God explains his displeasure to his people. They had been carrying out their call to religious observances and duties – they had been fasting, praying and keeping certain commandments. The problem was, though, that they had also been exploiting their workers, oppressing the poor, being unwelcoming to the stranger, ignoring the hungry and refusing to house the homeless. In other words, God is saying, 'Don't just look up at me; look across at my children as well.'

This passage also speaks directly to us today. If we are to call ourselves followers of Christ, it must make a positive, loving and life-affirming difference in our lives. If our faith makes a difference in our daily lives, it is priceless; if it does not, it is worthless. The reality is, of course, that all of us are too often like the Israelites in today's passage. We try desperately to follow our faith, but often end up getting our priorities completely wrong. The stand that we take as Christians on things we *think* are important blinds us to the things that really *are* important. Someone recently said to me how great it was that the church can still get on the front pages of newspapers in its defence of 'our beliefs and values'. But, unfortunately, the beliefs and values we are busy defending do not always reflect Jesus' teaching. The real message of the gospel, the message of liberation, grace, hope, peace and joy, often gets left behind. Sometimes I fear we are like the story of the Russian Orthodox Church in 1917 – while the revolution was raging all around them, they were holding a council to discuss liturgical colours.

God calls us to realign our priorities. Today's Isaiah passage reflects Jesus' identification with certain groups of people. In fact, scholars believe that Jesus told the parable in Matthew 25 with this Isaiah passage in mind:

> 'Lord, when did we see you hungry or thirsty or a stranger or needing clothes or ill or in prison, and did not help you?' He will reply, 'Truly I tell you, whatever you did not do for one of the least of these, you did not do for me.'
>
> MATTHEW 25:44–45

So, when we do live out our faith in our everyday lives and when we let our hour at church on Sunday infuse and enthuse the rest of our week, this is exactly what we will be doing – finding God in everyone we meet and treating them as if they were Jesus himself. That rather changes that phrase that we started with: 'Don't just look up; look across as well.' The paradox is that when we look across at our neighbours, we actually *are* looking up, because we are looking at Jesus. So, remember, don't just look up at him, but look across at him, too!

Reflection

The phrase that used to adorn many teenage bracelets in America – 'What would Jesus do?' – has almost become a parody. But that should not mask the importance of that very important question. Spend some quiet moments today reflecting on where Jesus' priorities would be channelled if he were living today. 'Don't just look up; look across as well.' Think of your own daily life – are there people we need to look across at today? Who are the people to whom we need to give our time, attention and resources?

Wednesday

Our call to recognise Jesus in ourselves

Before the coming of this faith, we were held in custody under the law, locked up until the faith that was to come would be revealed. So the law was our guardian until Christ came that we might be justified by faith. Now that this faith has come, we are no longer under a guardian.

So in Christ Jesus you are all children of God through faith, for all of you who were baptised into Christ have clothed yourselves with Christ. There is neither Jew nor Gentile, neither slave nor free, nor is there male and female, for you are all one in Christ Jesus. If you belong to Christ, then you are Abraham's seed, and heirs according to the promise.

GALATIANS 3:23–29

Recently, I officiated at the funeral of a congregation member. Derek was such a lovely man. He was a quiet and modest character. I thought I knew him well, but it was only when I visited him at home a few months before his passing that I heard more about his life. It was then I realised the quiet, and quite beautiful, impact that Derek's faith had on him and subsequently on the world around him.

Derek was working in sales in the Welsh steel industry when he won a scholarship with his company to undertake community work in Austria to build houses for refugees. He then returned to the UK to supervise the refurbishment of a school building for refugee children. After that, he felt he had a calling to social work, so he joined the Probation Service and remained there for the rest of his working life. Derek's impact on the young people on probation he helped went far beyond his own experience. In fact, I spoke to a number of people attending his funeral who, unbeknown to Derek himself, had completely turned their lives around due to his kind and caring influence.

Of course, not all of us can leave such an evident impact on the lives of those around us. However, our faith should still be having a positive and loving effect on everyday situations, on the world around us and on the people with whom we come into contact. In our passage today, the apostle Paul reminds us of our radical call to live in a way that reflects the life of Jesus. The uniqueness of first-century Christian baptism was that, as our passage states, converts were baptised 'into Christ'. The Jewish conversion ritual had no equivalent language. Paul is clear that, in baptism, we not only become one with each other, but also with Jesus.

A few years back, I attended a service in Llandaff Cathedral in Cardiff to celebrate 20 years of women priests in Wales. The preacher asked us to turn to the person next to us and trace the shape of the cross on their forehead. It was hugely moving, as it reminded us of our baptism and our calling to live as Christ did – bringing hope to our communities, peace to people's hearts and compassion to those who are suffering. We are, in baptism, marked with a cross, and while people can't see the actual cross that was left on our foreheads with oil and water in our baptism, they should see that cross reflected in our daily lives.

In the Eastern Orthodox Church, it is stated that we become *christoi* through baptism – in other words, that we become 'Christs'. In one of the recent films in the Star Wars franchise, *Rogue One* (2016), a blind character, Chirrut Îmwe, relies on the Force to know when to shoot or to avoid bullets. He repeats a phrase continually: 'The Force is in me; I am in the Force.' As I sat and watched the film in the cinema, I was amazed to hear that phrase, because it is reminiscent of a meditation I have used for many years to remind me of my call to live out Jesus in my everyday actions – 'Christ is in me; I am in Christ.' That is, in a nutshell, what being called by Jesus is all about.

Yesterday we considered the challenge to see Jesus in other people. Today, though, we are reminded that, by how we act and by what we do, people will see Jesus in us. We will be, as today's passage puts it, 'clothed' with Christ. As such, while there is certainly a place for talking about faith and discussing doctrine, in reality we connect with people in a far more profound way by reflecting Jesus in our acts of compassion and our seemingly inconsequential words and deeds of kindness.

When I left my childhood home to go to university to study theology, my dad gave me his Bible – it was the Bible that had been given to him by his own father when he had left for theological college. Inside the Bible were scribbled these words: 'Don't become of so much heavenly value that you are of no earthly use.' Our call to live out the gospel each day is at the very heart of our faith. As Albert Schweitzer put it, on reflecting on his Christian ministry as a medic:

> I wanted to be a doctor that I might be able to work without having to talk. For years I have been giving myself out in words... This new form of activity I could not represent to myself as being talking about the religion of love, but only as an actual putting it into practice.

Reflection

A prayer to be prayed slowly and mindfully – allow each word and phrase to inspire your walk with God:

Lord Jesus,
you call us to become more like you,
transform us into your likeness by helping us to recognise ways we
*   can reflect your love,*
while not all of us can do great things, through you, Lord, all of us
*   can do things with great love.*
In your name,
Amen

Thursday

The call to division

'I have come to bring fire on the earth, and how I wish it were already kindled! But I have a baptism to undergo, and what constraint I am under until it is completed! Do you think I came to bring peace on earth? No, I tell you, but division. From now on there will be five in one family divided against each other, three against two and two against three. They will be divided, father against son and son against father, mother against daughter and daughter against mother, mother-in-law against daughter-in-law and daughter-in-law against mother-in-law.'
LUKE 12:49–53

Recently, one of the exhibitions in the National Museum of Wales asked the question 'What do you want from life?' and then provided labels for people to write their answers. The answers from visitors from across the globe revealed something about contemporary values and priorities. Leaving aside my favourite answer ('Marry a ginger-haired person and have a baby called Chad'), a good number of the others simply stated they wanted to 'have fun', 'be happy', 'get rich' or 'be wealthy'.

In our passage today, Jesus was addressing a large crowd. I imagine they would have been shocked by what they heard. Scholars consider these to be some of the 'hard sayings' of the New Testament – the sayings that shock us, the verses that seem to go against what we think faith is about. Jesus tells his listeners that he has come to bring fire to the earth; he says that he has not come to bring peace, but division; he tells them that he has come to divide father against son, mother against daughter. What did Jesus, the Prince of Peace, mean when he said all this? Surely he is not calling us to conflict and division?

Before you rush away to pick an argument with the next family member you speak to, we must, of course, remember that the spirit and thrust of Jesus' teaching and life are calling us to live lives of peace, compassion and love. Rather than going against his call for us to live lives of love and peace, this seemingly shocking passage is, in fact, talking about the consequences of living out that very calling.

Jesus is here referring to the Old Testament. In the final chapter of Micah, the prophet predicts that divisions in families will happen when God's spirit is at work. In other words, God's call on our lives is so radical and revolutionary that it will lead to fracture, disagreements and division. In responding to the question from the museum, a Christian's answer will sooner or later clash with those whose answers are superficial, hedonistic or materialistic. After all, any strongly held views about what is important in life have the potential to divide people and to flare into disagreements. This is, to use a phrase from the singer-songwriter Billy Bragg, 'the sound of ideologies clashing'.

In our passage, Jesus is therefore talking about the natural consequences of loving our neighbours and recognising the ultimate value of all living things. He is calling us to get our priorities right. He is saying, very clearly, that faithfulness to him, living out his life of compassion, love and peace, must be the top of our priority list and, if it is, it will lead to clashes with others whose priorities are different.

Jesus certainly does not *want* division within households and families, but he knows all too well that following him will not mean a rosy, easy life – being his disciple has consequences. As a young man in the 1930s, my wife's great-grandfather recognised how Hitler's Third Reich was dehumanising people and this clashed with his deeply held Christian faith. As a result, it led to friction, division and conflict with family and friends. It was all a question of priorities. What did so many of them want from life? They would say to make their country great again – to rebuild its economic and military prowess, to help its people thrive and to reassert control of the future of their nation. What did he want from life? He wanted the radical message of God's love to shine through and touch the hearts of his people. He believed that making his country 'great' was not to do with control, wealth or military prowess, but with love, welcome and justice for the oppressed.

The truth is that developing our relationship with Jesus and fostering our spiritual life continues to demand that we make all sorts of moral and social stands, great and small. When we make justice and love priorities in our lives, then we are going to clash with those who have different priorities.

But when our views clash with those who prioritise prestige, power or possessions, we must not be disheartened. After all, the last chapter of Micah may warn of division in families, but the chapter does not end there. The Jewish people listening to Jesus 2,000 years ago would have known that Micah's prophecy finishes with a great hope for the future. Other Old Testament prophets and, indeed, Jesus' own life offers that same hope: 'The fruit of that righteousness will be peace; its effect will be quietness and confidence forever' (Isaiah 32:17). However alone we feel when we are prioritising Jesus' teaching of hope, love and peace, we must take heart – God's kingdom is breaking through all around us and, in the end, however bleak it might all seem, hope will triumph, justice will prevail and love will win.

Reflection

Take time to think about when you have had to take a stand on something. Where did you find the courage? What was the outcome? How do you feel about it all now, looking back? Pray to God to give you courage in the future and to keep you loving even those with whom you disagree.

Friday

The call to grace

The next day Jesus decided to leave for Galilee. Finding Philip, he said to him, 'Follow me.'

Philip, like Andrew and Peter, was from the town of Bethsaida. Philip found Nathanael and told him, 'We have found the one Moses wrote about in the Law, and about whom the prophets also wrote – Jesus of Nazareth, the son of Joseph.'

'Nazareth! Can anything good come from there?' Nathanael asked.

'Come and see,' said Philip.

When Jesus saw Nathanael approaching, he said of him, 'Here truly is an Israelite in whom there is no deceit.'

'How do you know me?' Nathanael asked.

Jesus answered, 'I saw you while you were still under the fig-tree before Philip called you.'

Then Nathanael declared, 'Rabbi, you are the Son of God; you are the king of Israel.'

Jesus said, 'You believe because I told you I saw you under the fig-tree. You will see greater things than that.' He then added, 'Very truly I tell you, you will see "heaven open, and the angels of God ascending and descending on" the Son of Man.'

JOHN 1:43–51

Recently, I had two conversations that made me reflect on today's passage. One was with a member of my congregation, who told me he'd once asked a vicar whether he really believed all the doctrines of our faith were true. The vicar looked sternly at him and barked back, 'I don't *believe* they're true; I *know* they're true!' The other conversation was with a vicar in training, and she said something very different. She told me her faith became stronger and stronger after, a few years earlier, she allowed herself to admit that she had some questions and doubts about her beliefs.

Today's passage does not relate the call to follow Jesus to being dogmatically certain about our beliefs. In fact, faith is not linked to believing any facts. Rather, faith is related to hearing and seeing – it is related to recognising something that is unique, uplifting and life-giving in the person of Jesus. When Philip persuades Nathanael to consider Jesus, he does not say, 'Come and believe in some doctrine' or 'Come and sign up to a creed.' He simply says, 'Come and see.' Our faith is about seeing truth – seeing the hope that Jesus offers to those who may have little hope in their lives and seeing the light that Jesus shines in places of despair and darkness. In other words, we are called to a way of seeing and a way of living, not primarily to a way of believing.

In the song 'The Box', the singer-songwriter Damien Rice suggests that, if love is a gift, then it cannot be allowed to box us in or become a set of rules. Love has to give us wings, rather than crush us with expectations. Listening to this song always reminds me of my faith. Christians believe that God's love is also a gift that we are offered. The Bible, though, should never be an ancient rule book that incarcerates us or boxes us in. Quite the opposite. The gift of God's love should free us to be truly human.

The apostle Paul expressed this in terms of law and grace. Our faith is not about rules, it's not about the law; it's about grace. In other words, it is about the freely given, unmerited love of God. Nowhere does Jesus call his followers to sign up to a set of doctrines. Faith is not a tick-list of things we need to believe. Our beliefs are certainly the foundation for our life-giving transformation, but our faith cannot remain locked up in our heads. Beliefs are only important in how they help us to 'see' Jesus, and, through seeing him, live out his love and justice.

There will be some who easily believe in the fine details of Christian doctrine, but others will cling on to the tenets of faith by their fingertips. There will be some who have seen the light and its glory will dazzle daily, but others will only be able to say, in the words of the former poet laureate Andrew Motion, 'I have seen the light – it flickers on and off like a badly-wired lamp.'

Sometimes the devout faith of others can carry us, just as we can carry them at other times. Bishop David Wilbourne recounts the time when he preached about certainty and doubt. At the end of the sermon, he asked his congregation to be truthful and, during the Creed, to stand if they definitely believed the line they were reciting and to sit down if they were unconvinced. Through the whole Creed he recalls people sitting down and standing up. At no point, though, was everyone sitting down or, indeed, everyone standing up. Christians carry each other through their beliefs, which is why we begin the Creed by stating 'We believe' rather than 'I believe'. After which, we leave our church buildings and, most importantly, we live out those beliefs in our everyday lives.

Whatever strength of faith we have – definite or doubting, firm or frail, certain or sceptical – it's okay either way. God loves us unconditionally, however certain we are or however many doubts we have. When it comes down to it, it is not about how convinced any of us are. To be called to follow Christ is not to absorb hand-me-down information or to be conformed into clones who believe exactly the same thing. There's always room for doubt and challenge. In fact, questions and doubts often result in learning and enlightenment.

Having doubts does not make us a heretic; having doubts simply makes us human. The real heresy is claiming to be a follower of Jesus but then not living out his love and compassion towards one another and the planet. Faith is about our attitudes and actions, our hope and vision. It's about delicately holding the joy and challenge of Jesus in a wonderful balance. It's about glimpsing the kingdom in our very earthly, difficult and draining lives. It's about opening our hearts to a God who cannot be contained in a creed or, indeed, in any human words. After all, our God, as we will celebrate at Easter, could not be contained in a box – or, indeed, in a tomb. Our God is a God of resurrection and new life. Jesus' call is, therefore, not a call to conformity. Rather, it is a call to transform our world through his love.

Reflection

A prayer to be prayed slowly and mindfully – allow each word and phrase to inspire your walk with God:

Lord of grace,
We thank you that our beliefs and doubts do not define who we are
  in your sight.
Although it is sometimes hard for us to accept, we know that we
  are fully accepted and loved.
Help us to live out your call to love genuinely, widely and wildly,
  whether or not our faith feels strong.
In Jesus' name,
Amen

Saturday

Memories

See, I have taught you decrees and laws as the Lord my God commanded me, so that you may follow them in the land you are entering to take possession of it. Observe them carefully, for this will show your wisdom and understanding to the nations, who will hear about all these decrees and say, 'Surely this great nation is a wise and understanding people.' What other nation is so great as to have their gods near them the way the Lord our God is near us whenever we pray to him? And what other nation is so great as to have such righteous decrees and laws as this body of laws I am setting before you today?

Only be careful, and watch yourselves closely so that you do not forget the things your eyes have seen or let them fade from your heart as long as you live. Teach them to your children and to their children after them.

DEUTERONOMY 4:5–9

The Jewish people have always used the past to inform and inspire the future. Great events like the Exodus, with Moses leading God's people out of Egypt, are constantly recalled in the Old Testament, especially when the Israelites are going through hardship. At the time of the exile, for example, Daniel and his fellow exiled Israelites would congregate by the rivers of the Euphrates and Tigris, telling each other stories of the past, weeping at what they had lost, reassuring each other that their God was still with them and looking with hope to the future. As Psalm 137 puts it, 'By the rivers of Babylon we sat and wept when we remembered Zion.'

On the morning of my last birthday, I found myself looking in the mirror. I saw grey hairs where they were once blond, lines on my face where there was once silky smooth skin and stubble that is now so white that my son recently begged me to grow my beard long so he could tell his friends that his dad was the real Father Christmas. This is not to mention how time is catching up with my back, my knees and my eyesight. Then I see how my children use social media like Snapchat and Instagram, and that's when I really feel old. The world is moving on so fast that we can often feel left behind and pine for a life we once had.

Our world is certainly a very different place from when many of us grew up. The temptation is, therefore, to focus on the past as a better and safer place – a place of community and unity, where it was easier to define what was good or bad, right or wrong. One of my favourite music albums is *The Kinks Are the Village Green Preservation Society* by The Kinks, originally released in 1968. On that concept album, Ray Davies, the songwriter, looks back longingly at his childhood and is desperate to reverse the clock and return to a simpler, happier time. Among the things he longs to return to are the local village green, Sunday school, fresh air, custard pies, billiards, Desperate Dan and china cups. Then, in one song, he meets an old friend called Walter, who has changed so much from their school days, and he soon realises that going back in time is not an option. We can't bring back the old days. But, he notes as he walks away from Walter, what we do still have is our memories. People change, things change, times change, but memories remain.

But what do we do, then, with these memories, with our nostalgia for the past? This is where scripture can teach us. The exiled Israelites, and indeed, later on, the grieving disciples, did not allow their memories of the past to make them small-minded, hateful or hurtful. In other words, our call as individuals is not to look at young people and say, 'We did it better in the past', and then criticise them or harangue them into our way of thinking. Likewise, our call as a country is not to isolate ourselves and look down on other people and other cultures. There is a difference between being inspired and uplifted by the past and wanting to return to the past. As a character in the film *Liberal Arts* (2012) puts it, 'Any place you don't leave is a prison.' So, like Daniel on the banks of the Tigris and like the disciples gathered in the upper room, our call is to use our memories to inspire, inform and build a more hopeful, compassionate and loving world.

There is, after all, something about heaven and eternity in our memories. C.S. Lewis writes about his childhood, when he built a toy garden with his brother. He knows he can't return in this life to that paradise lost, but his memory of that toy garden, he says, points to a future without suffering, worry or pain. It points to paradise regained. Until then, though, God can use our memories and nostalgia to inspire us to build something good *now* – so that, when the young people and children of today grow up, they will remember now as the 'good old days'.

Our God, after all, is not merely the God of the past. He is the God of the present and the future. So, as Christians, our call is not to complain and grumble about how things aren't what they used to be. Our call is not to be cynical and sceptical about the state of the world around us. Our call is certainly not to let our precious memories imprison us and impede us from moving forward. Rather, we need to be inspired, by both the Israelites in the Old Testament and the disciples in the New Testament, to use our past to inform and transform the present and to give us wonderful hope for the future.

After all, we Christians are people of hope who have faith in a God of transformation, a God who is, as the poet R.S. Thomas famously suggested, a fast God. Our call is to try, as best we can, to keep up with him. Our memories need not hinder us; rather, they can be the foundations on which we can build a kingdom of hope, love and peace – a kingdom of heaven on earth.

Reflection

Think back to a happy, joyful time in your life – it could be a period of your childhood or another time in your past. Enjoy your memories of that time – think of all the people and places that were special to you then.

To finish, commit to God that you will use the gift of that time in your life to bring God's hope and love to your community and your present relationships.

═══ **WEEK 3** ═══

Open our hearts
to your love

Sunday

Happiness

Is anyone among you in trouble? Let them pray. Is anyone happy? Let them sing songs of praise. Is anyone among you ill? Let them call the elders of the church to pray over them and anoint them with oil in the name of the Lord. And the prayer offered in faith will make the sick person well; the Lord will raise them up. If they have sinned, they will be forgiven. Therefore confess your sins to each other and pray for each other so that you may be healed. The prayer of a righteous person is powerful and effective.

JAMES 5:13–16

Recently, I was given a three-month sabbatical from work, and planned exciting journeys to the Orkneys, Lindisfarne, Sheffield and London. Unfortunately, a reoccurrence of a back injury put an end to all that. The journey of recovery that I faced was far from the travels I had expected.

In the Bible, characters rarely embark on joyous and easy journeys – we don't read stories of Moses on an uplifting family holiday or Elijah having fun nights out with his friends. Instead, they are often thrown into journeys they didn't expect by challenges, disaster or grief. The conclusion of those travels is never that they discover happiness through escaping their troubles. Rather, through those turbulent journeys, God's love transforms and heals. Sometimes characters even change their names to show such a transformation – Abram becomes Abraham; Simon becomes Peter; Saul becomes Paul. It is not that God is a sadist who throws us into times of despair, but, when we do face hardships, he stands alongside us and is able to give us a hope that the world alone cannot give us. This challenges us and changes us.

Yet our world often views happiness as our ultimate attainment – as the one thing that will lift us from our misfortunes. Most of us know that chasing happiness will invariably lead to frustration or disappointment, but our default is still to try to do anything we can to grasp happiness and avoid unhappiness. It's so built into our nervous system that our quest for happiness seems as natural as breathing air. My youngest son learnt very early on that he gets presents and tasty, sugary treats on his birthday and Christmas Day. In other words, he was guaranteed happiness on those two days. So, from a young age he would come into our bedroom and ask excitedly, 'Is it my birthday or Christmas today, Daddy?' The way his little smile would suddenly disappear when I told him it was neither of those days made me realise he was basically living for two days of happiness a year, and 363 days of disappointment!

This desire for happiness, this worshipping of pleasure, doesn't stop as we grow older, but continues apace. I've started taking a shortcut to the shops from my house, through a patch of woodland. It's a beautiful little walk, except for one thing – each evening dozens of empty energy drink cans are left behind by young people chasing a little hit of happiness. None of us is immune to this chase. We may not enjoy the kick of energy drinks ourselves, but we may, for example, be lifted daily by the little shots of dopamine in our brains every time our mobile phones ding. In fact, businesses and companies build fortunes on manipulating our minds to believe that happiness should be our ultimate aim. Fast food outlets entice our children with 'happy meals', just as pubs and bars urge us adults to take advantage of their 'happy hours'.

When we face difficulties or tragedy, we realise how futile this race for happiness is. In our passage today, James writes to the early church communities, encouraging them to support those who face troubles, worry or illness. In his letter he commends supporting others with compassion and love, but also with prayer, so our attention is continually with those who are facing troubles.

God does not offer a quick fix for our troubles, whether we are facing grief, illness, relationship difficulties, depression, anxiety or unemployment. But he does reassure us of our ultimate worth in his sight and, as a result, he helps us to make peace with our suffering and unhappiness.

Not that this is an easy thing to do. In fact, when we face hardships, all we want to do is get through to the other side as quickly as possible. Yet our journeys are often long and frustrating. Travelling through the recent pandemic showed us that. Sometimes it may seem as if we can see no light at the end of the tunnel. But that is because the tunnel is never straight. Instead, it winds and bends, and that is what guarantees we will be very different people when we arrive at the light. What we go through will always remain part of us, but, if God can help us make peace with our difficult times, it is these experiences that lead us to love – they are what help us to stand alongside others, either through direct help or prayer. We become wounded healers, transformed through our journey, and we are able to offer the love that strengthened us in the midst of our troubles to others who are struggling now.

Reflection

Take a moment of silence to consider what you've been through, however long your journey in darkness has been or continues to be. Think of how your experiences have already helped others and could help share God's love with others in the future. Pray in your heart that you are given strength, first, to reach out to others to ask for love, support and prayer and, second, to reach out to others to offer love, support and prayer.

Monday

God loves mis-shapes

On the third day a wedding took place at Cana in Galilee. Jesus' mother was there, and Jesus and his disciples had also been invited to the wedding. When the wine was gone, Jesus' mother said to him, 'They have no more wine.'

'Woman, why do you involve me?' Jesus replied. 'My hour has not yet come.'

His mother said to the servants, 'Do whatever he tells you.'

Nearby stood six stone water jars, the kind used by the Jews for ceremonial washing, each holding from eighty to a hundred and twenty litres.

Jesus said to the servants, 'Fill the jars with water'; so they filled them to the brim.

Then he told them, 'Now draw some out and take it to the master of the banquet.'

They did so, and the master of the banquet tasted the water that had been turned into wine. He did not realise where it had come from, though the servants who had drawn the water knew. Then he called the bridegroom aside and said, 'Everyone brings out the choice wine first and then the cheaper wine after the guests have had too much to drink; but you have saved the best till now.'

What Jesus did here in Cana of Galilee was the first of the signs through which he revealed his glory; and his disciples believed in him.

JOHN 2:1–11

Some years ago I organised a large confirmation service at which our bishop presided. I took many hours typing out the order of service, before printing it and photocopying it. It was only when the service started and we began to sing the first hymn that I realised an embarrassing mistake. I had, in hastily cutting-and-pasting a section, left a letter out of the final line of the first hymn. So, we began the service by all joining in the hymn which, instead of asking, 'Lord, let us sing', petitioned God to, 'Lord, let us sin'!

In our passage today the organisers of the wedding really messed up. This miracle is often considered for its symbolic importance, with the new 'choice wine' representing Jesus himself. At a more basic level, though, the miracle represents Jesus' offer of hope at our times of need. Running out of wine at a wedding might not sound disastrous. However, in first-century Palestine the wedding banquets would last a whole week and if anything went wrong it brought disgrace on the families of the bride and groom. Today, if a wedding party ran out of wine, people might moan and grumble a while. But in Israel 2,000 years ago, it was a serious offence to fail in your hospitality duties.

In our own ways, I'm sure we can all relate to these wedding arrangers. We all make mistakes and get things wrong. Sometimes these mistakes are small, but sometimes they can have serious consequences. When we mess up, it can embarrass, depress and worry us. This is where Jesus steps in, as he did at that wedding in Cana. He may not change the situation itself, but he can certainly change the way we view the situation. A disastrous mistake can become an opportunity, just as a wasted chance can lead to something useful. That can be as liberating as if Jesus had miraculously changed the situation. After all, he helps us to view our mistakes as He views them – with love, understanding and forgiveness.

Sometimes, in facing our blunders, we are hard on ourselves, judging ourselves in a way we rarely judge others. At other times, our mistakes can reveal that we care too much about how we appear to others. Our egos become dented and that is the real reason for our upset. Then, of course, there are the times when our reaction to our mistakes, whether that is anxiety, anger or embarrassment, is rooted in a desire to always be in control. Being a perfectionist is never an easy life, as we attempt to iron out all our own mistakes and judge others harshly for theirs.

When I was a child, I adored chocolates that were called mis-shapes. These were all the chocolates that had gone wrong in the factory. The fact they were not perfect made me love them even more – each pack was unique and, when I opened them, I never quite knew what I was going to get. In some way, all of us reflect these chocolates. Most of us are broken and none of us are perfect. But we are all unique, and many possibilities and opportunities can spring from our imperfections. Most important of all is the fact that, even if we don't live up to the expectations of others and ourselves, God loves us for who we are. All of us are mis-shapes, but we must never forget that I am not the only one who loves mis-shapes – God loves mis-shapes too!

Reflection

Think of a time you have made a mistake, when you said or did the wrong thing. As you leave this incident with God, take time in stillness and silence to thank God for loving you, whatever mistakes you have made. Then commit yourself to loving others whatever mistakes they have made. Ask Jesus to help you see others through his eyes.

Tuesday

Love for all creation

This is the account of the heavens and the earth when they were created, when the Lord God made the earth and the heavens.

Now no shrub had yet appeared on the earth and no plant had yet sprung up, for the Lord God had not sent rain on the earth and there was no one to work the ground, but streams came up from the earth and watered the whole surface of the ground. Then the Lord God formed a man from the dust of the ground and breathed into his nostrils the breath of life, and the man became a living being.

GENESIS 2:4–7

The native American word *wetiko* is from the Cree tribe and describes a disease. The native American scholar Jack D. Forbes tells us that 'for several thousands of years human beings have suffered from this plague, a disease worse than leprosy, a sickness worse than malaria, a malady much more terrible than smallpox'. *Wetiko* is the disease of cannibalism. It is not, though, referring to eating human flesh. Rather, it refers to eating the life and soul of others through selfish greed. We suffer from *wetiko* when we regard our needs and our wants to be more important than those of others around us. Forbes puts it this way: 'It is the consuming of another's life for one's own private purpose or profit.' Native Americans believe Europeans took this disease to different parts of the world, including over the Atlantic, and, as it is a contagious illness, it started to infect other cultures. By now, this disease has reached epidemic proportions.

Wetiko is the polar opposite of what our faith should be. Our faith teaches us that love, in the forms of relationship, care and cooperation, should be the driving force of our actions. This is true of our dealings with other people, but it is true also in our dealings with other living things and the environment around us. From the very first chapters of Genesis, we're shown that there is unity and harmony to every part of God's creation. The Hebrew word for 'man' (*adam*) is closely related to the word for 'dust', 'soil' or 'ground' (*adamah*). From the very beginning, we have been part and parcel of nature itself, made from soil and destined to return to soil. Furthermore, in Genesis 1, everything is created before humans – wind, water, earth, air, fish, birds and animals – and when we're finally formed, we're created for being in relationship with both God and the world around us. Jewish theologian Martin Buber summarised this in the words 'In the beginning was relationship.'

So our relationships with the world around us echo God's essential being. Buber claims that whenever we are engaged in the process of relationship, whether with other human beings or with nature, we are connecting with God. After all, God is love, and love is at the very heart of relationship. The concept of the Trinity brings this home to us forcefully. As Screwtape, a senior demon, writes to his less-experienced demon nephew in C.S. Lewis' *Screwtape Letters*: 'He claims to be three as well as one, in order that this nonsense about Love may find a foothold in His own nature.' God is not about *wetiko*. God is not about earthly power, domination and authority. Jesus' life and death showed us that God is about servanthood and giving up power to stand alongside us in our suffering and struggles. We need to move away from viewing God as powerful, judgemental and demanding, and recognise the God of union, love and harmony.

This should inspire our own dealings with the world around us. Our faith's emphasis on the importance of loving relationships gives us a cure for *wetiko*. Despite this, the reality is that it is difficult for even people of faith to be healed from this disease. Our world often sees competition as more important than cooperation, and rivalry as more important than relationship. And we go along with this, often without even realising how radically at odds it is with our faith.

To move away from *wetiko*, we must recognise that society, and the world at large, is one large family, with everything having a place and purpose. Relationship is at the heart of everything. Even at the level of quantum physics, the entire fabric of all that exists is woven so closely that everything is intricately related. We humans are part and parcel of the wonderful web of life, and even ordinary objects in the environment around us, such as plants, flowers, pets, trees or birds, can become symbols to us of the unity of our vast universe. These living things are not merely 'useful' to us, and they are certainly not objects to be devoured, consumed and exploited as part of our *wetiko* greed. Rather, they are things that hold value and significance in themselves.

However tempting it is to see nature in terms of what *we* can get out of it, nothing in our world must be dismissed as cheap and disposable – not any of our fellow humans, whoever they are or whatever they've done, nor animals and the natural world around us. God does not call us to control the cosmos. Instead, he calls us to embrace his beautiful and liberating cure for our *wetiko*, and to extend his limitless love towards *all* of his creation, with no exceptions.

Reflection

Our faith challenges us to make sure we are in a living, loving relationship with the everyday things we experience in our world. Take some time today to feel connected with the natural world – if you cannot get outside to the countryside or to your local park, spend some time feeling connected with your garden, with a pet or even with your houseplants. Thank God for the gift of the world around us.

Wednesday

God of the losers

Now when Jesus saw the crowds, he went up on a mountainside and sat down. His disciples came to him, and he began to teach them.

He said:

'Blessed are the poor in spirit,
   for theirs is the kingdom of heaven.
Blessed are those who mourn,
   for they will be comforted.
Blessed are the meek,
   for they will inherit the earth.
Blessed are those who hunger and thirst for righteousness,
   for they will be filled.
Blessed are the merciful,
   for they will be shown mercy.
Blessed are the pure in heart,
   for they will see God.
Blessed are the peacemakers,
   for they will be called children of God.
Blessed are those who are persecuted because of
   righteousness,
   for theirs is the kingdom of heaven.

'Blessed are you when people insult you, persecute you and falsely say all kinds of evil against you because of me. Rejoice and be glad, because great is your reward in heaven, for in the same way they persecuted the prophets who were before you.'
MATTHEW 5:1–12

I vividly remember my first school sports day as a parent. It was a beautiful, sunny day, and everything was set for a lovely afternoon. Unfortunately, no one had mentioned to me there is an unspoken code of conduct for sports days. It came to my daughter's race and she shot out in front, leading girls almost twice her height. I was so proud. But, then, as the finishing line approached, she started to slow down and didn't see one of her classmates catching up fast. I panicked and started screaming, 'Come on! What are you playing at? Faster, faster!' I continued shouting louder and louder, becoming more and more animated. My daughter sped up and did, indeed, cross the finishing line in first place. I screamed a big 'That's ma girl!' and fist-pumped the air. I turned around to see all the other parents staring at me in disbelief. Finally, one could not hold back any longer. 'Calm down, mate,' he said. 'It's not the bleeding Olympics!'

From an early age, our society tells us that our very worth is in our actions. What we do and how well we do it define who we are. After all, when we meet someone, the first thing we enquire about, after their name, is what they do, and most of us are impressed, even if only quietly, if the answer involves success and achievement. It is really hard to rewire our minds to stop considering winning and succeeding as the ultimate aim, as I discovered at that school sports day.

Anthony de Mello, the Jesuit contemplative, tells a story about a woman who was in an accident and found herself in heaven, facing a great light. Suddenly she heard a great, booming voice ask, 'Who are you?' She gave her name. The voice answered, 'I didn't ask your name, I asked who you are.' She said, 'I'm a school teacher.' The voice answered, 'I didn't ask for your profession, I asked who you are.' She said, 'I'm the wife of the mayor.' The voice answered, 'I didn't ask whose wife you are, I asked who you are.' She said, 'I'm the mother of four children.' The voice answered, 'I didn't ask whose mother you are, I asked who you are.' By this point the woman was finding herself rather confused. But the voice asked again, 'Who are you?' She said, 'I'm a Christian.' The voice answered, 'I didn't ask for your religion, I asked who you are.' She said, 'I'm the one who prays regularly, who goes to church, and reads the Bible.' The voice answered, 'I didn't ask for your religious practices, I asked who you are.' She said, 'I'm the one who gives to charity, the one who helps the poor and needy.' The voice answered, 'I didn't ask about your charitable giving, I asked who you are.' It was then the medics revived her. The story ends with her leaving her hospital bed, determined to spend the rest of her life finding out who she really was.

It is interesting to think about how we ourselves might answer that question – 'Who are you?' It's an important question because how we see ourselves also defines how we view others and, indeed, how we treat others. If we define ourselves by our successes, achievements or appearances, we'll also look at others and judge them by the same values. In our minds, their worth will be based on superficial, outward factors – what work they do, how they look or how successful they are.

As Christians, we are challenged to look beyond this. Today's passage shows how the love-filled value system of the kingdom of God subverts the value system of the kingdoms of money, prestige and power. After all, Jesus does not affirm those who are successful or wealthy, but instead champions the poor in spirit, the persecuted, the powerless, the peacemakers, the pure of heart, those who mourn, the meek, the merciful and those who hunger and thirst for righteousness.

In other words, our God is not the God of the winners. God is, in the eyes of the world, the God of the losers. This goes so radically against our upbringing and instinct that it sounds plain wrong to our ears – God is the God of the losers. 'The last will be first, and the first will be last', as Jesus put it (Matthew 20:16). This is at the crux of our faith. 'Crux', of course, is the Latin word for cross, and the cross certainly reflects this. Jesus lived in poverty, was persecuted and hated, was subject to violence and torture, wielded no power or worldly authority, and cared little for the success that the world values so much. Instead, he lived to serve others through his ultimate sacrificial love. As he put it, 'Greater love has no one than this: to lay down one's life for one's friends' (John 15:13). The cross was a sign that, in worldly terms, Jesus was a loser. But, of course, the cross was not the end of the story – the loser became the winner, the rejected became the worshipped and the crucified became the resurrected.

Reflection

Like the woman in Anthony de Mello's story, consider the question 'Who are you?' Either on paper or in your head, list the answers you might give. Our identity is an important part of our lives, but our call is to look beyond superficial labels. As Christians, our identity must be rooted, first and foremost, in God's love for us and for others. Commit yourself to seeing both yourself and others through the loving eyes of Christ.

Thursday

Nobody is a nobody

After this, Jesus travelled about from one town and village to another, proclaiming the good news of the kingdom of God. The Twelve were with him, and also some women who had been cured of evil spirits and diseases: Mary (called Magdalene) from whom seven demons had come out; Joanna the wife of Chuza, the manager of Herod's household; Susanna; and many others. These women were helping to support them out of their own means.

LUKE 8:1–3

Our passage today is the first mention in Luke's gospel of Mary Magdalene, who journeyed alongside Jesus, was there at his crucifixion and was one of the first to encounter the risen Christ. Yet the church has often given Mary a scandalous backstory that is not actually found in the Bible. Recent scholarship has strongly questioned this portrait. Scholars now believe Mary was a strong, independent woman who supported Jesus spiritually and even financially. As a witness to the resurrection, she stood up forcefully for justice and truth, at a time when women's testimony was too often ignored. As an article in *The Independent* newspaper put it in 2017, 'If there's a feminist figure from the Bible for the #MeToo era, it could very well be Mary Magdalene.' The Roman Catholic Church has even recently declared a feast day for Mary that is on a par with those of the twelve disciples.

Mary Magdalene's role in the gospel stories, alongside those of other women who followed and supported Jesus, fits well with the heart of Jesus' teaching – a teaching which championed love, justice and equality. Both the Jewish tradition and the Roman system of the first century saw some individuals and groups as having little worth or value – women, children, slaves, people with skin diseases, widows, divorcees, tax collectors, those of a certain nationality or race, and so on. The message of Jesus stood in stark contrast to these attitudes. He taught a radical message that viewed everyone, whatever their status or background, as precious and loved children of God. For him, no one was expendable, useless or worthless. As the apostle Paul put it, 'There is neither Jew nor Gentile, neither slave nor free, nor is there male and female, for you are all one in Christ Jesus' (Galatians 3:28).

It is tempting to think that our own world is vastly different from the first century, but we must remember that this beautiful but radical message of Jesus also stands in stark contrast to attitudes of our own time. As the #BlackLivesMatter movement has reminded us, we also have various groups of people who are regarded as having less value than others – those who still face barriers economically, politically and socially.

As Christians, we need, first, to recognise and overcome our own prejudices; and, second, to stand up and oppose those powers that erect barriers, whether individuals, businesses, institutions or governments. In other words, we need to be living out the revolutionary message of our faith – that every single person is a loved and precious child of God and every individual is uniquely valuable, whatever their social background, gender, age, sexuality, race, nationality, disability or faith, and whatever violence, harassment or prejudice they have been subject to. *Nobody* is a nobody. We are so used to seeing reality TV programmes with people competing to be a 'somebody', that we forget the timeless message that Jesus taught that *everybody* is a somebody.

When the whistle was blown at the end of the 2018 football World Cup final, the winning French players immediately ran towards the bench and celebrated with the whole squad – the players, the substitutes (a few of whom had not played a single minute of the tournament), the manager, the coaches, the physios, the team doctor and the strategists all celebrated together. There was a real recognition that this achievement was not simply the accomplishment of the eleven players who started the final game. Rather, winning the World Cup was the achievement of many, many people, on and off the field and over a long period of time.

In our lives too, everybody plays their part, everybody has a role. And each of our roles, whoever we are, whatever our backgrounds and whatever we do, contributes to the larger picture. Each day we bless other people's lives, often in ways that we will never know. Each day others touch our lives, often in ways they won't realise. *Nobody* is a nobody. *Everybody* is a somebody. Each person is a child of God. We are all uniquely valuable and loved by him, and we are used by him daily to bring about his loving and compassionate will. When Jesus was baptised, heaven was torn open and a dove descended on him. These words were heard: 'You are my Son, whom I love; with you I am well pleased' (Mark 1:11). God, the loving Father, is saying to each of us those same words: 'You are my child, whom I love; with you I am well pleased.'

Reflection

Often we find certain people easy to admire and appreciate, while others seem to fall beneath our notice. Think of someone in your life who isn't necessarily a prominent, charismatic figure, but who has nevertheless been a quiet, positive and loving presence for you, standing alongside you and supporting you. Thank God for what this Mary Magdalene figure has brought to your life and commit yourself to also being a steady, loving presence in the lives of others.

Friday

God loves us!

Later they sent some of the Pharisees and Herodians to Jesus to catch him in his words. They came to him and said, 'Teacher, we know that you are a man of integrity. You aren't swayed by others, because you pay no attention to who they are; but you teach the way of God in accordance with the truth. Is it right to pay the poll-tax to Caesar or not? Should we pay or shouldn't we?'

But Jesus knew their hypocrisy. 'Why are you trying to trap me?' he asked. 'Bring me a denarius and let me look at it.' They brought the coin, and he asked them, 'Whose image is this? And whose inscription?'

'Caesar's,' they replied.

Then Jesus said to them, 'Give back to Caesar what is Caesar's and to God what is God's.'

And they were amazed at him.

MARK 12:13–17

In Greek mythology, Theseus was a young warrior who sailed from Athens to Crete to battle with the Minotaur, the monster with the head of a bull and the body of a man. When he returned, the Athenians preserved his ship. But as the years passed by, the ship naturally started to rot. So, bit by bit, each rotting part of the ship was replaced with new material. After a few hundred years the mast, the sails, every single plank and all the ropes had been replaced. This left a question that philosophers have argued about for centuries – after replacing every part of the boat, was this still Theseus' famous ship?

This might sound like a pointless question, but it is, in fact, at the heart of being and reality. Recently, I was visiting my parents' house and looked at photos of myself as a child. As I looked at the face of a mischievous, smiling boy, I remembered the story of the ship of Theseus and asked myself – was I the same person as the one in those photos?

On one hand, I obviously am. But, on the other hand, I've changed so much since those photos – could it be that I'm actually a completely different person by now? After all, human cells don't last a lifetime and our bodies constantly regenerate themselves – the lining of our gut is replaced every five days; red blood cells every 120 days; and our bones every 10 years. Physiologically at least, almost nothing of little Trystan is writing these words.

Furthermore, I also have a very different view of the world than I did then, with regards to society, politics, faith and even, sadly, about Father Christmas and the Easter Bunny. I've changed because of education, but also because of what I've experienced, not least the pain and suffering that I've had in my own life and that I've witnessed in the lives of friends, family and parishioners. So, the question remains – in what ways can I be regarded as the same as the small child in those photographs?

In today's passage, Jesus asserts, 'Give back to Caesar what is Caesar's, and to God what is God's.' It was an answer that flummoxed the Pharisees who were trying to catch him out – to get him either to support paying taxes to the Romans, and thus seal his fate with the Jewish people, or to suggest that people refuse to pay taxes, and thus seal his fate with the Romans. His answer was profound. It is an answer that allows us to recognise that we give money to our government when we pool our resources for roads, schools and hospitals, but also acknowledges that *all* things, including ourselves and each other, are gifted to us from our Father. Caesar's image may have been on first-century coins, just as our monarch's head is on ours, but God's image is on *everything*.

Jesus' answer is an invitation to recognise the image of God in all his creation, including in you and me! This leads us Christians to recognise and affirm the true nature and reality of our being. After all, in the first chapters of Genesis, God creates humankind in his own image and, on looking back at his handiwork, we are told that he 'saw all that he had made, and it was very good'. In other words, we are all children of God. He created us, and he delights in us. However far down the tunnel of darkness we have fallen, however different we may be from our childhood selves, in God's eyes we still continue to be unique, irreplaceable and infinitely loved.

Scientists looking at a picture of Little Trystan and then looking at the person writing this might point to the cerebral cortex in my brain. This is the one part of my body that will remain for my lifetime, storing up memories, thoughts, views and attitudes. Scientists might claim that this is what makes Big Trystan the same as Little Trystan. Our passage today urges us to go beyond a simply mechanistic reading of reality. It allows us to affirm that, as everything is God's, so each one of us has ultimate worth and value.

We are who we are because we are created and loved beings – we are God's children, made in his image and loved as much now as when we were innocent little children (or, in my case, not so innocent). After all, whatever joys and sufferings we have experienced in our lives, however different our bodies, views and attitudes might be from when we were children, that one thing hasn't changed – God's boundless, unconditional and forgiving love for us all. That, more than anything, should have a huge impact, first, on how we view ourselves, loved and cherished as we are, and, second, on how we treat others, loved and cherished as they are.

Reflection

George Orwell asked what do you have in common with your five-year-old self? 'Nothing,' he concluded, 'except that you happen to be the same person.' Think of yourself when you were younger – some of your hopes, dreams, desires, dislikes and fears. It may be helpful if you look at an old photo of yourself while you are thinking. Now think of all that you've been through – joy, pain, happiness and suffering. At this point, you might find looking at yourself in the mirror will aid your reflection. How different are you now than you were as a child? Take some time and silence to sit in the knowledge of God's love for you through all the ups and downs of your life.

Saturday

Equality

A certain ruler asked him, 'Good teacher, what must I do to inherit eternal life?'

'Why do you call me good?' Jesus answered. 'No one is good – except God alone. You know the commandments: "You shall not commit adultery, you shall not murder, you shall not steal, you shall not give false testimony, honour your father and mother."'

'All these I have kept since I was a boy,' he said.

When Jesus heard this, he said to him, 'You still lack one thing. Sell everything you have and give to the poor, and you will have treasure in heaven. Then come, follow me.'

When he heard this, he became very sad, because he was very wealthy. Jesus looked at him and said, 'How hard it is for the rich to enter the kingdom of God! Indeed, it is easier for a camel to go through the eye of a needle than for someone who is rich to enter the kingdom of God.'

LUKE 18:18–25

Growing up in Wales, we would be reminded every week by our maths teacher that it was a Welshman, Robert Recorde from Tenby in Pembrokeshire, who invented the equals sign (=). Only a year later, he was arrested for debt and died in prison in Southwark in 1558 at only 46 years old. Maybe this Welsh link was part of why I grew to love maths in school. There was especially a satisfaction in seeing the equals sign with the correct number on the other side of it, and, of course, a big tick next to it. But if that equals sign was incorrect, if one side of the sum did not 'equal' the other side, then that was frustrating and unsatisfying.

Today's passage challenges us to consider equality and how we react to inequality in our society. Do we just ignore the huge inequality between rich and poor in our society, or are we uncomfortable and frustrated, appalled even, when we look at people's lives and see that the sums of economic wealth do not equal each other?

According to Barack Obama, inequality is the defining issue of our time. There was actually a decline in poverty and inequality after World War II, but this soon began to change and, in recent years, poverty in the UK has been almost three percentage points higher than it was when the Child Poverty Action Group was formed in 1965. From the 1980s onwards, the gap between those with the greatest wealth and those with the least grew wider and wider. By today, hierarchies that were accepted only a generation ago are now thankfully denounced – divisions between gender, race and sexuality. A hierarchy of rich and poor, though, is seen as perfectly acceptable and, to some, even sensible.

As Christians, we need to ask how Jesus might view the present situation. Today's passage is a huge challenge to us all. Perhaps, like the rich man in the story, there is one thing we lack. If we take seriously Jesus' talk of the kingdom of God, then we need to reassess our society's obsession with money and we must take seriously the needs, cares and concerns of others, not merely our own. After all, in the gospels the kingdom of love is a kingdom of parity and equality, as many of Jesus' parables demonstrate (not least the parable of the workers in the vineyard; Matthew 20:1–16).

Even in worldly terms, research shows that a move towards equality improves society generally. Countries with better social and economic equality see a higher quality of well-being, socially and individually, than more unequal countries. In other words, a more equal society sees everyone's lives improving, both rich and poor. Crime, ill health, obesity, depression and anxiety are all lower in countries where the equality gaps are smallest, irrespective of overall wealth. 'The truth is,' wrote Richard Wilkinson and Kate Pickett in their book *The Spirit Level:*

Why equality is better for everyone, 'that both the broken society and the broken economy resulted from the growth of inequality.'

In our passage today, Jesus challenges a young man to replace the kingdom of Mammon in his life with the kingdom of God. This is such a difficult step to take that both the young man himself and countless others down the centuries have failed to live out this call. In fact, historically, scholars have, whether consciously or not, even watered down Jesus' revolutionary challenge. It has long been claimed that 'the eye of the needle' was a narrow gateway in Jerusalem that camels had to unload their goods in order to pass through, just as a rich man has to unload his material possessions. Recently, though, scholars have questioned the existence of such a gate. The interpretation now is that, in Aramaic, the word *gamla* probably meant thick rope, rather than camel, and so Jesus is saying that it's easier for a thick rope to get through the eye of a needle than for excessive and unequal wealth to have anything to do with the kingdom of God. In other words, for money to be part of God's kingdom is almost an impossibility.

There is something profoundly radical about this attitude to wealth. It is a challenge to us all. Jesus knew something that sometimes we just don't want to face. Wealth is not the way to peace of heart, to a healthy and happy society, nor to a peaceful world. In 1988, as our society was beginning the journey to its present inequality, the Church of England bishops met with the government to express their concerns. The politicians argued that freedom was important in Christianity and so economic freedom was absolutely essential, as it relates directly to our individual liberty. The normally reserved Bishop Michael Baughen of Chester then cut through the discussion. 'I'm afraid you misunderstand, Prime Minister,' he said. 'Christianity is not about freedom; it's about love.' Equality is at the very heart of Christian love.

Reflection

The Trussell Trust, which works with people of all faiths and none, is an anti-poverty charity founded on Christian principles. It opened the first food bank in the UK in 2000 and now supports a network of food banks providing emergency food for those in crisis. The charity considers its 'founding verse' to be Jesus' words in Matthew 25:35: 'For I was hungry and you gave me something to eat.' Take some food to your local food bank collection point. Alternatively, find out about volunteering in your local food bank or explore the Trussell Trust website and consider donating money to the charity. Finally, take some time in prayer to ask God for a society where food banks are unnecessary.

=== **WEEK 4** ===

Open our ways to your will

Sunday

Signs and wonders

Some time after this, Jesus crossed to the far shore of the Sea of Galilee (that is, the Sea of Tiberias), and a great crowd of people followed him because they saw the signs he had performed by healing those who were ill. Then Jesus went up on a mountainside and sat down with his disciples. The Jewish Passover Festival was near.

When Jesus looked up and saw a great crowd coming towards him, he said to Philip, 'Where shall we buy bread for these people to eat?' He asked this only to test him, for he already had in mind what he was going to do.

Philip answered him, 'It would take more than half a year's wages to buy enough bread for each one to have a bite!'

Another of his disciples, Andrew, Simon Peter's brother, spoke up, 'Here is a boy with five small barley loaves and two small fish, but how far will they go among so many?'

Jesus said, 'Make the people sit down.' There was plenty of grass in that place, and they sat down (about five thousand men were there). Jesus then took the loaves, gave thanks, and distributed to those who were seated as much as they wanted. He did the same with the fish.

When they had all had enough to eat, he said to his disciples, 'Gather the pieces that are left over. Let nothing be wasted.' So they gathered them and filled twelve baskets with the pieces of the five barley loaves left over by those who had eaten.

After the people saw the sign Jesus performed, they began to say, 'Surely this is the Prophet who is to come into the world.'

JOHN 6:1–14

When I suffered a recent reoccurrence of an old back injury, the pain was excruciating, and my mind started dwelling on how bleak the future seemed. After a particularly dark few days, I lay in my bedroom, in pain and frustrated. I looked outside and there, on the telephone wire, staring at me, was a goldfinch. I hadn't seen one for a long time, perhaps even years. For a brief moment, my worries faded and I was entranced by this beautiful visitor. As it flew away, I reached down for my iPad and, for some reason, I googled 'What is the meaning of seeing a goldfinch?' I was immediately faced with dozens of classical paintings of Jesus holding goldfinches. It turns out that there has long been a link between faith and the goldfinch, and it was even believed that the bird got its red face from trying to remove Jesus' crown of thorns. I then read that, down the years, the goldfinch was regarded as a bird of healing.

There I was, in pain and despair, and I was visited by a traditional icon of healing and hope. Was that just a coincidence? Did God somehow send that goldfinch? Was it God who prompted me to google the meaning of this small bird? I am not sure about any of those things, but I do know that God spoke to me through that goldfinch. I do know that my life was opened to his kingdom of hope and joy through that small bird. To me that goldfinch became a sign. It became a source of hope, at a time when I felt only hopelessness. It became a beacon of light, when all I was seeing was darkness. It became a glimpse, however faint, of joy, when all I was feeling was pessimism and despair.

Today's passage is one of the seven miracles in John's gospel. But John does not call these events 'miracles'. Instead, these wonder stories are referred to by the Greek word *semeia*, which is translated 'signs'. In fact, some scholars think that, when writing his gospel, John may have used a separate, earlier document, known as the 'signs source', which contained all seven of these signs. Whether John used such a document or not, one thing is certain – the stories are hugely important to him. To him, they show who Jesus really is and what he brings to us and reveals to us. It is, though, only people whose eyes were open to noticing God's will amid the ordinariness of their lives who recognised the significance of these spiritual moments. I'm sure there were many who were so busy stuffing their faces at the feeding of the 5,000 that they missed the wonder of that sign, just as I'm sure there were many at the wedding in Cana, where Jesus changed water to wine, who were too busy making merry to marvel at that moment. 'Unless you people see signs and wonders, you will never believe', Jesus said (John 4:48).

As Christians, our call is to open our eyes to see those signs that God's kingdom is here – to open our ways and journeys to God's will. After all, in our oh-so-busy lives it's too easy to miss those moments of grace, those glimpses of heaven around us, those moments when God's will is being revealed to us. The psychologist Carl Jung claimed that 'modern people don't see God because they don't look low enough'. In other words, it's not always the big things that reveal God's will and presence. Sometimes he's in the small details, in the goldfinches. Jung even had a word for these moments or events where meaningful coincidences happen – 'synchronicity'.

Such moments in the ordinariness of our everyday lives, those goldfinch moments, are the 'signs' that God's kingdom is all around us. Not that they are easy to recognise, especially when we face times of suffering, pain or grief. But these are shafts of light in the darkness of our struggles. By opening ourselves to God's will in the small and seemingly insignificant details of our everyday lives, a path of hope is illuminated and our journey can be transformed.

Reflection

A prayer to be prayed slowly and mindfully – allow each word and phrase to inspire your walk with God:

> *God of the everyday,*
> *we know that you come to us disguised in our lives,*
> *help us to take time daily to glimpse you in the apparent*
> *ordinariness of our existence,*
> *inspire us to open our ways, emotions and decisions to the light of*
> *your loving will.*
> *In Jesus' name,*
> *Amen*

Monday

Discerning God's will

'The days are coming,' declares the Lord,
  'when I will make a new covenant
with the people of Israel
  and with the people of Judah.
It will not be like the covenant
  I made with their ancestors
when I took them by the hand
  to lead them out of Egypt,
because they broke my covenant,
    though I was a husband to them,'
      declares the Lord.
'This is the covenant that I will make with the people of Israel
    after that time,' declares the Lord.
'I will put my law in their minds
  and write it on their hearts.
I will be their God,
  and they will be my people.
No longer will they teach their neighbour,
  or say to one another, "Know the Lord,"
because they will all know me,
    from the least of them to the greatest,'
      declares the Lord.
'For I will forgive their wickedness
  and will remember their sins no more.'

JEREMIAH 31:31–34

How strangely people would be viewed if they spoke like the Old Testament prophets, peppering 'declares the Lord' or 'thus says the Lord' into their conversations. Admittedly, it would be useful around the house, if the children weren't doing what they were told to do – 'Thus sayeth the Lord, thou shalt go up and brush thy teeth' or 'Thus sayeth the Lord, thou shalt use more frequently please and thank you.' Yet, in reality, if anyone was to claim that they were speaking directly from God in this way, we would be very suspicious of them, to say the least.

The prophet Jeremiah lived in Israel around 2,600 years ago, at a time when atrocities were happening in the country, not least the horrific practice of sacrificing children to foreign gods. This is the context and background to Jeremiah hearing the voice of his loving and just God and communicating God's message to his people. Even the word 'prophet', which is from the Greek words *pro*, meaning 'in place of', and *phemi*, meaning 'to speak', refers to this communication – God speaks to Jeremiah and he, in turn, listens, hears and then speaks to others in God's place, reminding them of what God's love is demanding of them and, in our passage today, promising a new covenant, which will liberate and transform hearts and minds.

Prophets are not unique in having God speak to them. After all, the question is not whether God talks to us; rather it is whether we are listening. Communication should always be two-way. Any relationship, whether with a friend or family member, could not develop, and certainly could not thrive, if the communication was only one way – in fact, it would cease to be a 'relationship' if one person were talking all the time and the other one listening.

Our culture, though, is obsessed with words. Whether face to face or on social media, people are constantly using language to battle with others, trying to win arguments or change minds. But words are not truth in themselves – they are merely our ways for expressing experience, feelings or thoughts. Jeremiah was a poet, using words to bring to God's people his wonderfully transforming message – connecting to their emotions and imaginations. When God speaks to us, though, he can do so in a plethora of ways. Sometimes he does come to us through words (through the Bible or through something someone tells us or suggests), but he can also communicate with us through experiences, feelings, people, events and so on.

In fact, sometimes words even get in the way of us discerning God's will in our lives. The 1980s pop group Depeche Mode sang about words doing violence to silence. Life, after all, is about more than words. There was a time when we were young when none of us could speak and that did not make our lives any less valuable. Similarly, there may be a time in the future when, due to illness or age, we may not be able to speak again – and again our lives will be no less valuable. However much some Christians will try to persuade us otherwise, we are not people of the book. The word of God to Christians is not a book – the Word is God's personal communication and, of course, the Word became a person. The Bible is the word of God because it communicates, and is a witness to, that Word. As the prologue to John's gospel puts it: 'In the beginning was the Word, and the Word was with God, and the Word was God' (John 1:1). As Jesus is the Word, when we experience in our lives echoes of that transforming covenant of love that Jeremiah looks forward to, then God is communicating with us.

So, our call is to discern when that communication is happening – in experiences, feelings, actions and events, as well as in things people say to us or things we hear. Christians do not put these down to coincidence. Neither do we put them down to blind fate. Instead, we hold that God's providence is always at work in our lives. In other words, we hold that God is always communicating, prompting us to carry out his loving will. When we do this, we are aligning ourselves to what theologian Hans Urs von Balthasar called the 'theodrama', the story God wants to tell, rather than our own personal 'egodrama'. After all, it is when we are discerning the path of love in our everyday lives that we are, like the prophets of old, hearing God speak to us.

Reflection

A prayer to be prayed slowly and mindfully – allow each word and phrase to inspire your walk with God:

> Living Lord,
> sometimes all we have is words, sometimes all we have is silence;
> help us to listen for you, however you reveal yourself to us.
> Open our ears, eyes, thoughts and feelings to recognising your
>   voice,
> and give us the gift of clarity in our discernment of what you are
>   saying and how your will is prompting us to walk your path of
>   transforming love.
> In Jesus' name,
> Amen

Tuesday

Idols

**Jesus and his disciples went on to the villages around Cae-
sarea Philippi. On the way he asked them, 'Who do people say
I am?'**

**They replied, 'Some say John the Baptist; others say Elijah;
and still others, one of the prophets.'**

**'But what about you?' he asked. 'Who do you say I am?'
Peter answered, 'You are the Messiah.'**

Jesus warned them not to tell anyone about him.

MARK 8:27-30

The book *American Gods*, written by Neil Gaiman and later adapted as
a popular television series, considers the question of where we place
value in our lives. It pictures our lives as a war between the old gods
of religion and belief and the new gods in which we have started to
put our faith. At one point in the story, the god Odin speaks to the
old gods, reminding them that they have been usurped from their
thrones and replaced with new gods that are now worshipped. 'As
all of you will have had reason plenty to discover for yourselves,' he
booms, 'there are new gods growing, clinging to growing knots of
belief: gods of credit card and freeway, of Internet and telephone, of
radio and hospital and television, gods of plastic and of beeper and of
neon; proud gods, fat and foolish creatures, puffed up with their own
newness and importance.'

Even 2,000 years ago people had to choose their loyalties and
priorities – in other words, they had to decide who to worship. In
our passage today, Jesus asks his disciples what people are saying
about him. Peter eventually confesses that Jesus is the Messiah. The
significance of the location of this episode is sometimes overlooked.
The episode took place at Caesarea Philippi on the slopes of Mount

Hermon, 25 miles north of Galilee. It was a city that was famously steeped in paganism. In the Old Testament period it was an important town for worshipping the idol Ba'al. Later, under the Greeks, the city was called Paneas, as the shrine to the Greek god Pan was located there. Finally, for the Romans, it was called Caesarea Philippi – Philippi after Philip the Tetrarch, a puppet king of the emperor, and Caesarea after Caesar himself, who was seen as a divine figure in the empire. So, the context of this episode is that the disciples were affirming the lordship of Jesus in a place that reminded them that there were many other idols fighting for their devotion. These idols were, quite literally, other divine figures.

Today, though, it is quite different 'idols' that demand our time and attention, as *American Gods* illustrates. In fact, it could be said that, in our world today, it is not atheism but idolatry that is the greatest enemy of God's will. By making something an idol, we replace Jesus as the most important thing in our lives, and so absolutely anything can become an idol to us. As Christians, we should be proclaiming with Peter that Jesus is the Messiah. We should be affirming that living out his will and his message of peace, hope, love, forgiveness and social responsibility is more important than anything else to us. Our faith demands that we give ourselves up to something that is beyond ourselves. God's will must take priority in our lives.

With idolatry, though, the idol, which reflects our own wants and desires, takes the centre stage, and so it is our personal will that domi-nates our ways. Life becomes all about 'me' and what is important to me. We start to champion what gives us comfort and makes us feel good, safe and happy, despite the fact that lasting freedom, fulfilment and joy are not to be found in these things. We become slaves to finance (money or credit cards), possessions (houses, cars or electrical goods), status (what people think of us) and our appearance (how we look to others), which are all things that only offer fleeting and temporary comfort.

At the end of today's passage, Jesus tells his disciples not to tell any-one that he is the Christ. In biblical scholarship, this instruction has become known as the 'Messianic secret'. Scholars maintain he did this because he knew that the Israelites were looking for a very different Messiah. They were looking for a political figure to start a revolution against Rome. In other words, they were looking for an idol, for some-thing that they believed suited and benefited them. Jesus, though, led his disciples away from the pagan centre of Caesarea Philippi – he refused to be made into an idol. Instead, he led them to Galilee and on to Jerusalem. The consequence of that journey for all of them was, of course, great suffering – he himself was crucified and eleven of the twelve disciples were martyred for their faith. But the journey ulti-mately brought fulfilment and great glory. As the Spanish poet Miguel de Unamuno put it, 'May God deny you peace but give you glory.'

In other words, giving up our idols does not guarantee us a calm and settled life. Jesus wants us to follow him away from Caesarea Philippi and towards Galilee and even to Jerusalem. That journey can be pain-ful. It's not easy to give up our selfish wants and longings, especially as our society has persuaded us that it is only natural and normal to desire money, possessions, status and praise. But for us to affirm, with Peter, 'You are the Messiah', we are expected to take the journey that the disciples took. By doing so, we affirm, 'Your kingdom come, your will be done', rather than 'My will be done'; we move from darkness to a life of colour, hope and fulfilment; we embrace love, compassion and social justice; and we become more like Jesus himself.

Reflection

Be as truthful as you can by considering the question: what are my own personal idols that I need to fight against each day? Lay those battles before Jesus and affirm that he is the Messiah, the Son of the Living God.

Wednesday

Standing together

Just as a body, though one, has many parts, but all its many parts form one body, so it is with Christ. For we were all baptised by one Spirit so as to form one body – whether Jews or Gentiles, slave or free – and we were all given the one Spirit to drink. And so the body is not made up of one part but of many.

Now if the foot should say, 'Because I am not a hand, I do not belong to the body,' it would not for that reason stop being part of the body. And if the ear should say, 'Because I am not an eye, I do not belong to the body,' it would not for that reason stop being part of the body. If the whole body were an eye, where would the sense of hearing be? If the whole body were an ear, where would the sense of smell be? But in fact God has placed the parts in the body, every one of them, just as he wanted them to be. If they were all one part, where would the body be? As it is, there are many parts, but one body.

1 CORINTHIANS 12:12–20

I am from a large family – I have three brothers and one sister. I tease my parents by saying they kept trying until they got a child they liked. All five of us siblings look quite similar, but we're actually very different people, with different personalities, jobs and hobbies – I love visiting prehistoric monuments; my sister plays in a brass band; one brother has represented Wales internationally in birdwatching; another brother has his favourite football team, Shrewsbury Town FC, tattooed on his arm; and my youngest brother was a finalist in the Welsh version of the talent show *The X Factor*. Despite our similar upbringings, we each have our own unique and precious characteristics that I know our parents love and cherish.

It dawned on me recently how our families reflect the church. From the time of the disciples, groups of Christians have thought and acted very differently. Even the early Christians in the book of Acts, for example, disagreed about whether they should be practising Jewish customs. By today, all of us Christians are distinct in the ways we worship, in our priorities and in our theology. But we are, of course, similar in one important way – we all pray to God as *our* Father. So, each of us is a brother and sister in Christ. Our unique and precious characteristics, which our Father in heaven loves and cherishes, should bind us together, rather than tear us apart.

The five of us Hughes children were brought up in the beautiful Snowdonia National Park in north Wales. My grandparents, who lived in the big smoke of our capital city, Cardiff, used to call us the feral mountain children, and I quite often tease my own children by saying that I was raised by wolves on the slopes of Mount Snowdon. While we were not wolf pups, we did fight like cats and dogs – over everything and anything! I remember one punch-up with my older brother that began with an argument as to who was the most famous – the 50s rock-and-roll star Jerry Lee Lewis or the singer-songwriter Suzanne Vega. Twenty years later, I'm still certain I was correct. (It's clearly Jerry Lee Lewis.) By now, though, those kind of childish arguments are in the distant past and, despite our different personalities, we all get on remarkably well and enjoy meeting up regularly.

Again, just as brothers and sisters go through changes in the way they treat each other as they grow and mature, so the relationships of our churches have developed. Five hundred years ago, Christians were burning each other at the stake in Britain, and even a century ago there was so much hatred, bitterness and prejudice on all sides. My doctoral research centred on church relationships in Wales during the 20th century. I remember trawling through old newspapers in dusty archives and being shocked at what I was reading – local chapel members pelting Catholic priests with stones as they walked by; Anglican bishops denouncing all other churches in Wales as intruders; and Catholics claiming those outside Rome were consigned to hellfire. We are used to saying that things have changed for the worse, so we should rejoice and thank God for this change for the better – our churches have grown up and matured. Although there may be still, sadly, some examples of antagonism between churches, many Christians now lovingly recognise each other as brothers and sisters. It is especially heartening to see concrete signs of different traditions working together to bring the love, peace and hope of Jesus to local communities – joint social justice ventures, shared buildings for worship and innovative educational schemes.

Still, we must never take relationships for granted. God's will is towards unity and harmony. As our passage today puts it, 'we were all baptised by one Spirit so as to form one body – whether Jews or Gentiles, slave or free – and we were all given the one Spirit to drink'. Furthermore, this unity will not survive without effort. Good relationships require time and kindness. I am close to my siblings because we phone and visit each other, we text each other and we try to remember each other's birthdays (although there are now a lot of nieces and nephews to also remember). Likewise, God wills us to nurture our relationships with our brother and sister Christians by affirming each other, visiting each other and praying for each other. By doing so, we can let others know that religion is not something that divides but something that brings us together and gives mutual support and love. After all, we are all parts of the body of Christ, and, as Psalm 133 announces, 'how good and pleasant it is when God's people live together in unity!'

Reflection

Phone or send a text/email to a Christian that you know from another church or denomination, telling them how much you appreciate them. Alternatively, find some other way of showing them your appreciation. Then spend some time in prayer, bringing before God those brothers and sisters in Christ who have supported you in the past or who continue to support your journey as a disciple of Jesus.

Thursday

Hyperbole and consequences

'If anyone causes one of these little ones – those who believe in me – to stumble, it would be better for them to have a large millstone hung round their neck and to be drowned in the depths of the sea. Woe to the world because of the things that cause people to stumble! Such things must come, but woe to the person through whom they come! If your hand or your foot causes you to stumble, cut it off and throw it away. It is better for you to enter life maimed or crippled than to have two hands or two feet and be thrown into eternal fire. And if your eye causes you to stumble, gouge it out and throw it away. It is better for you to enter life with one eye than to have two eyes and be thrown into the fire of hell.'

MATTHEW 18:6–9

When I was growing up my dad had numerous phrases that would annoy me – 'This house is lit up like a Christmas tree'; 'Money doesn't grow on trees'; and 'If your friend put their hand in the fire would you put in yours?' The one that used to infuriate me more than any other, though, was, 'How many hundreds of times have I told you not to exaggerate?'

Now that I'm older, and preaching and writing is what I do for a living, I realise the dramatic importance of hyperbole. Exaggeration is not always a good thing, and can even lead to us to deceit or lies. But, as long as we recognise that this technique is being used, it can be helpful and effective. Even as a child, I knew that money didn't literally grow on trees, but the phrase taught me something about the value of not squandering what we have. I never literally saw a friend put his hand into a fire, but the phrase taught me to resist peer pressure. Leaving my bedroom light on doesn't literally look like dozens of sparkling lights on a Christmas tree, but the phrase helped me to recognise the impact that wasting electricity has on the environment.

Today's reading is graphically violent if we take it literally – people with millstones tied around their neck getting thrown into the sea or having their eyes plucked out and their hands and feet cut off. Jesus, though, came from a Jewish writing and speaking tradition that was steeped in the technique of hyperbole. 'You are all together beautiful, my darling; there is no flaw in you', asserts Song of Songs 4:7. I'm sure Solomon's beloved was gorgeous, but even the very best of us have a couple of flaws. By Jesus' time, hyperbole, metaphor and pictorial language were techniques used by rabbis, the teachers of the day. Jesus, though, had a particular way of employing these techniques effectively to grab his audience's attention or to shock them into recognising the deep truth he was asserting. As G.K. Chesterton put it, 'Christ had even a literary style of his own... the diction used by Christ is quite curiously gigantesque – it is full of camels leaping through needles and mountains hurled into the sea.'

In using the technique of hyperbole, Jesus didn't want us to take him literally. After all, the literal fulfilment of today's reading wouldn't achieve the desired goal anyway. One of my closest and oldest friends has been blind since he was a teenager, and I remember once discussing this passage with him. 'Believe me, Trystan,' he said sipping his pint of beer. 'Tearing someone's eyes out won't stop them lusting.'

While they shouldn't be taken literally, Jesus' hyperbolic statements should still be taken with utmost seriousness. Today's passage teaches us something radical about God's will and how our ways should be transformed by following him. Everything we do, Jesus is telling us, has profound effects on both others and ourselves. Violence, prejudice, greed, selfishness and objectifying others – they all have unhealthy consequences. Likewise, our deeply held opinions that we think are perfectly justifiable, but which actually go against Christ's call for love and care of all, have far-reaching consequences. At the heart of this passage, then, is a call to treat each other with respect, care and kindness.

Jesus' exaggerated statements are certainly not trying to make us feel guilty or to hate ourselves. Instead, they are trying to encourage us to recognise the radical nature of God's kingdom and the impact God's will should have on our way of thinking and acting. Our faith challenges us to look *outside* ourselves at the problems of the world around us, but also *inside* ourselves at our own personal issues, be they lust, anger, envy, hatred, selfishness or material greed. How we think and how we act in our daily lives has an impact, not only on our own well-being, but also on other individuals, on our society and on our environment. If we really want to challenge the world, we must start with challenging ourselves. And if we really want to change the world, we must start with changing ourselves.

Reflection

Take some time to consider your innermost thoughts and emotions. Be open and truthful with yourself about any struggles you have to control – lust, anger, envy, hatred, selfishness or greed. Be kind to yourself about your inclinations, but ask Jesus to help you transform yourself daily into his image.

Friday

Give them hope

Now the tax collectors and sinners were all gathering round to hear Jesus. But the Pharisees and the teachers of the law muttered, 'This man welcomes sinners, and eats with them.'
Then Jesus told them this parable: 'Suppose one of you has a hundred sheep and loses one of them. Doesn't he leave the ninety-nine in the open country and go after the lost sheep until he finds it? And when he finds it, he joyfully puts it on his shoulders and goes home. Then he calls his friends and neighbours together and says, "Rejoice with me; I have found my lost sheep." I tell you that in the same way there will be more rejoicing in heaven over one sinner who repents than over ninety-nine righteous people who do not need to repent.'

LUKE 15:1–7

I read a story recently about a woman who became convinced that there was too much hatred, injustice and prejudice in her community. She decided to try to change the people there. Night and day, she would walk around the streets, protesting against greed, indifference and selfishness. At first, people listened for a while before simply walking on. Eventually, they just stopped listening. Despite this, the woman continued protesting for years until, one day, a small child approached her and said, 'You poor woman. You shout and you scream, but can't you see that it's all hopeless?' The woman agreed that it seemed hopeless. 'So, why are you still doing it?' asked the child. 'Well,' replied the woman. 'In the beginning I thought I could change people; now I'm just determined not to let people change me.'

Sometimes our temptation will be to give up on discerning and following God's will. The world can be cynical and disparaging about faith and spirituality, and we can be dragged down into dismissing our discernment of God's communication. Today's passage is a parable of mercy, grace, compassion and love. It reassures us that no one is beyond redemption – God will not give up on us. It is also, however, a parable of hope. Ninety-nine sheep are safe, but the good shepherd's concern turns to the one lost sheep. We, therefore, have a beautiful example of a shepherd who does not give up hope, despite the difficulties he faced. While this parable reassures us, it can also inspire us. It can, after all, encourage us to stay strong in our own beliefs and not give up hope ourselves, whatever the obstacles in our way. And, of course, the knowledge of a God who is so determined to share his unlimited love with others, however lost they seem, gives us a beautiful hope that we can also share with others.

When Lesslie Newbigin, the theologian and missionary, came back to Britain in the 1970s after many years living in India, he was asked what he found most difficult about returning to his home country. He did not choose to complain about how secular the country was becoming or to talk about the loss of Christian values in contemporary Britain. Instead, he spoke about a phrase that holds as much, if not more, truth today – 'the disappearance of hope'. Our faith, after all, is about hope – hope for *all* people, whatever their background, race or age. In other words, like the woman in the story, we must not become disillusioned and let our hearts of hope be changed. Each of us must continue to discern and live out God's will, and together we must offer a hope that our communities, society and world desperately need.

The social activist Harvey Milk, one of the first openly gay people to be elected to public office in the United States, inspired those who felt they had no voice and saw little hope for the future. There continue to be many people today in our communities who feel that way, because of their social background, age, sexuality, race or simply because of the labels that others put on them. Our call as Christians is to give them hope. By doing so, we align ourselves with God's will. Within a year of Harvey Milk giving his famous hope speeches, he was gunned down and killed. Living out and preaching a kingdom of hope is not always going to be easy for us either. Our faith, after all, means sacrifice – it is the religion of the cross. But it is also a religion of the rainbow, the dove, the light, the life-giving water and the resurrection. As such, we Christians and our churches should be inspired by Harvey Milk's famous words:

> You have to give them hope. Hope for a better world, hope for a better tomorrow, hope for a better place to come to if the pressures at home are too great. Hope that all will be all right. Without hope the 'us's' – the downtrodden, the oppressed, the struggling, the suffering – without hope the 'us's' just give up. I know that you can't live on hope alone, but without it, life is not worth living. So you, and you, and you, have got to give them hope.

Reflection

Consider how you personally, or how your church (if you attend one), could help bring hope to a person or a group of people. Think about which group is most in need in your local community, and try both to pray for them and to do something practical to help them.

Saturday

Using our imperfections

But we have this treasure in jars of clay to show that this all-surpassing power is from God and not from us. We are hard pressed on every side, but not crushed; perplexed, but not in despair; persecuted, but not abandoned; struck down, but not destroyed. We always carry around in our body the death of Jesus, so that the life of Jesus may also be revealed in our body. For we who are alive are always being given over to death for Jesus' sake, so that his life may also be revealed in our mortal body.

2 CORINTHIANS 4:7–11

Recently, I decided to brave the wind and the rain to go in search of a famous prehistoric standing stone in the south Wales valleys. Most standing stones simply have 'standing stone' written on an OS map, but this one was special – it had its own name: Maen Catwg. From the train station, I walked over three miles to get to the stone and got absolutely soaked, but I was quite sure it would be worth it. In my imagination, it was going to be big and imposing, like a Welsh Stonehenge. When I finally arrived at the field, I immediately saw it was not a 'standing' stone at all. Rather, it was a flat stone in a muddy field. I can't say I was overwhelmed!

But then I walked up to the stone, and it turned out, despite its appearance from afar, to be fascinating. The most amazing thing about it was what at first seemed to be its imperfections. Most Neolithic standing stones have no clear features on them and nothing inscribed. This stone, though, had around 40 strange circular holes in it – like cup holders in a car. The holes had been skilfully carved into the stone up to 4,000 years ago. Scholars maintain that they represented the early farmers' belief that, first, farming life is cyclical – that the seasons come and go – and, second, that life is cyclical, as we pass from this life to the next. These holes, and all they represent, were truly beautiful. Because of these 'imperfections', a boring stone in a field became a prehistoric awe-inspiring work of art.

My little adventure got me thinking about what God wills for our lives. Each and every one of us have done things we regret in the past. Each and every one of us have also been through so much in our lives – illness, grief, sadness, pain and loss. We're broken people. Like the holes in the Neolithic stone, all of us have what may seem like imperfections. But our faith teaches us the good news that we don't need to be perfect. God is not in the business of expecting perfection. In fact, when we go through moments of regret and times of difficulty, he can transform our imperfections. He can bring us hope and resurrection. Furthermore, once we're out of the other side of whatever we're going through, it is our imperfections that are often the things that make us beautiful and more useful and empathetic to others.

Our society may tell us that we have to be perfect, but God wants us to recognise that it is our holes, carved and chiselled into our topsy-turvy, up-and-down lives, that can give us strength and beauty. In our passage today, the apostle Paul describes us as jars of clay. Such jars, seemingly worthless in themselves, were used in the ancient Near East to conceal treasure. Paul is saying that we, as clay jars, are where God's treasures are stored. Our own vessels may be frail and broken, but God is able to use our weakness to bring his treasures into this world. In other words, God transforms our imperfections into blessings – we are all his beautiful works of art.

When I visited the Navajo communities in New Mexico, I was shown beautiful stitched rugs. One weaver explained to me that if any of them weaved the perfect rug, they would interrupt just one stitch so it did not remain perfect. True beauty, he said, needs some imperfection. As the singer-songwriter Leonard Cohen put it – everything has a crack in it, and this is how the light can get in.

When my son was a toddler, each night I would read a children's storybook Bible to him. When we would get to the resurrection story, he would look at Jesus, glorious in his resurrected body, and stroke the nail wounds on his hands, saying, 'Poor Jesus.' All of us have our own nail wounds, from difficult times that we have faced in the past. We'll always be frail, cracked and imperfect; we'll always be jars of clay; we'll always have our own unique marks chiselled into us. But that's what makes me 'me', and that's what makes you 'you'. The wonderful thing is that our God is a God of resurrection, and he uses our brokenness and imperfection to sow his transformational seeds of love in our world.

Reflection

God wills us to make peace with the fact we are jars of clay – frail, broken and imperfect. Take some time to think about the difficult times you have faced. In silence, lay these times at the foot of the cross and ask God to use our lives as they are, lives of both joy and suffering, to help others experience his kingdom.

=== **WEEK 5** ===

Open our actions to your compassion

Sunday

Radical love

As Jesus and his disciples were leaving Jericho, a large crowd followed him. Two blind men were sitting by the roadside, and when they heard that Jesus was passing by, they shouted, 'Lord, Son of David, have mercy on us!'

The crowd rebuked them and told them to be quiet, but they shouted all the louder, 'Lord, Son of David, have mercy on us!'

Jesus stopped and called them. 'What do you want me to do for you?' he asked.

'Lord,' they answered, 'we want our sight.'

Jesus had compassion on them and touched their eyes. Immediately they received their sight and followed him.

MATTHEW 20:29–34

The documentary film *All or Nothing: Manchester City* charts the premiership-winning 2017–18 season of Manchester City football club. At the midway point of the season, one of their star midfielders, David Silva, is going through a distressing time in his family life – his son Mateo has been born prematurely, at 25 weeks, and is being kept in hospital in Valencia. With Silva at his son's bedside, the team plays an important match against Tottenham Hotspur, who are also contenders for the league title. Manchester City manager Pep Guardiola inspires his team with a rousing monologue reminding them of their teammate's situation: 'Today you have to win for one reason. You have to win for David Silva and his girlfriend Jessica. He is suffering with life. If you go out there and you enjoy, you enjoy it for him. And if you go out there and you suffer, you suffer for him.'

In recent years, appeals for us to have more compassion for others have been made from various quarters – social commentators on our

TV screens, self-help books on our shelves and politicians on their campaign trails. Yet compassion is not simple to define. In Guardiola's words to his team, though, we hear something of what compassion means – to suffer with those who are suffering and to rejoice with those who are joyful. After all, the root of the English word 'compassion' is the Latin *compassio*, meaning 'to suffer with'.

Our passage today describes Jesus as showing compassion to the blind men. The Greek word used (*splanchnitzomai*) implies a deeply felt and radical reaction – it could be translated literally as 'moved to his guts'. In other words, compassion is a deep-seated and radical form of love that demands we truly share the suffering of those who are struggling.

Compassion, then, is not just a buzzword to be used when it is convenient for politicians, journalists and commentators to try to show how much they care. Instead, compassion is a challenge to each and every one of us to feel the pain of what others are going through. In a society that seems obsessed with competition and wealth, our call is to champion compassion as the only currency that matters. For Christians, it should be at the heart of how we treat each other and act towards the world around us. Still, while entrepreneurial skills are taught in schools to children as young as six and seven, compassion is rarely seen as an important aspect of educational policy. And while successive governments talk about compassion in the NHS, nurses and doctors feel that they are forced to sideline it in favour of finance and targets. And while our hearts go out to migrants and refugees who might lose their lives in the bid to reach our country, compassion is certainly lacking in much of the anti-immigration rhetoric we hear in some quarters of the press or media.

The reality is that true compassion is rarely in evidence in the institutions that hold sway in our land. Finance, wealth and power seem more important than reaching out to the marginalised and disadvantaged. Our society can be individualistic, materialistic and self-serving. Worse still, we have been made to believe that it is weak and naive to champion love, kindness and compassion over material prosperity, egotism and competition.

As Christians, we must resist this attitude. Jesus knew that love has nothing to do with weakness or naivety. On the very night he was tortured and murdered, he said, 'My command is this: love each other as I have loved you' (John 15:12). His crucifixion and resurrection gave us that promise that love and compassion can bring profound change.

But we cannot expect it to come from outside us – from Westminster, the City or Fleet Street. Change needs to start in our own hearts. 'The kingdom of God is within you,' asserts Jesus (Luke 17:21 – see NIV footnote). God's kingdom starts inside and then grows outwards. Like throwing a pebble into water, it is the kingdom of ever-increasing circles.

Likewise, compassion starts in our heart, and then grows outwards, enveloping more and more people, bringing hope and transforming futures. If we are compassionate in our daily lives, we will see the kingdom of God break through into our communities – bringing light to places of darkness, love to those who suffer prejudice or disadvantage, and hope to those who think they have no future.

Reflection

Consider some of the people we are called to be compassionate towards: the migrant, the person visiting a food bank, the person on benefits, the disabled, the homeless, the unemployed, the prisoner, the sick in hospital, the terrified teenager who's just found out she is pregnant, the worker struggling on minimum wage and the elderly care-home resident who has no visitors. Are we really moved to our guts with compassion? Do we really feel the pain and struggle others are facing? Keep such groups and individuals in your prayers and consider ways you might help them practically, perhaps through committing some of your time or money to helping them.

Monday

The compassionate Samaritan

He asked Jesus, 'And who is my neighbour?'

In reply Jesus said: 'A man was going down from Jerusalem to Jericho, when he was attacked by robbers. They stripped him of his clothes, beat him and went away, leaving him half-dead. A priest happened to be going down the same road, and when he saw the man, he passed by on the other side. So too, a Levite, when he came to the place and saw him, passed by on the other side. But a Samaritan, as he travelled, came where the man was; and when he saw him, he took pity on him. He went to him and bandaged his wounds, pouring on oil and wine. Then he put the man on his own donkey, brought him to an inn and took care of him. The next day he took out two denarii and gave them to the innkeeper. "Look after him," he said, "and when I return, I will reimburse you for any extra expense you may have."

'Which of these three do you think was a neighbour to the man who fell into the hands of robbers?'

The expert in the law replied, 'The one who had mercy on him.'

Jesus told him, 'Go and do likewise.'

LUKE 10:29b–37

Having young children in the house introduces you to all sorts of strange and colourful TV programmes with some intriguing names, such as *Twirlywoos*, *Hey Duggee*, *Messy Goes to Okido* and *Rastamouse*. My youngest son's favourite show, though, is not so new-fangled – it's the old classic *Tom and Jerry*. He avidly watches the original series from the 1940s and 1950s. Most *Tom and Jerry* episodes have the two enemies competing against each other. Several of them, however, have the cat and mouse working together to overcome obstacles. My son's absolute favourite episode is the one he calls 'the baby one', where the couple join together to care for a little infant who gets into all sorts of scrapes. On his insistence, our household have watched that episode on a continual loop for the past year.

You might think that we have all become tired of this one *Tom and Jerry* episode, but, in fact, the care and compassion shown by our two heroes towards a helpless baby has provided a welcome break on the vicarage TV screen from the toxic atmosphere of much of the political debate on news and discussion programmes. Worst of all is hearing the weakest of our communities denigrated and derided by some commentators and politicians. Our passage today is a real challenge to us as we consider some of the rhetoric that we have heard from both sides of the Atlantic in recent years. We are, after all, called as Christians to model the Good Samaritan, and not to be like the priest and the Levite, turning our heads to look the other way when we see injustice or hear bigotry.

Jesus, of course, never referred to the Samaritan with the word 'good', but the phrase 'Good Samaritan' still has a long history of many centuries. Today, the word 'good' is rather insipid and bland, being used in rather mundane ways, like when a dog collects a stick you've thrown or when a toddler eats their greens – 'Good boy! Good girl!' In light of this fact, perhaps we should rechristen the parable as the 'Compassionate Samaritan'. After all, the Samaritan in the parable was someone who truly enters the suffering of his neighbour, actively standing alongside a stranger in need and doing all he can to alleviate that suffering.

It is natural to think of Jesus himself as the Samaritan, as he offers healing and wholeness to those whose wounds he sees and whose cries he hears. But the incarnation leads us also to see him as the wounded, dying man on the road to Jericho (Matthew 25:40). Jesus enters the suffering of the distressed and depressed. Our call is not only to see him as the answer to the world's pains, but also to recognise him in its suffering – in the eyes of the mother at the food bank, of the refugee pleading for hospitality, of the migrant who feels unwanted and alienated by the rhetoric of hate, and of the poor, disabled, grieving and ill. Our role is to see Jesus in each and every person and be ready to offer our own compassion and care to them, whoever they are.

And yet too often our world is blind to the unique beauty and worth of each person. Instead, we are persuaded to consider what is best for us personally and thus see ourselves in opposition to others. Such fear and self-centredness were the response of the priest and the Levite in this parable. Yet the compassionate Samaritan did not consider first what was in it for him. Neither did he calculate the dangers of stopping to help. And he certainly didn't check whether the beaten body at the side of the road was a different nationality, gender or race to himself. Likewise, our own call when we face those who are suffering and troubled is not to ask what is best for us. Rather, we simply need to ask what's the most compassionate thing to do. Only then will healing break through hostility, peace through prejudice, freedom through fear and hope through hate.

Reflection

A prayer to be prayed slowly and mindfully – allow each word and phrase to inspire your walk with God:

> Lord of compassion,
> you teach us that we are meant for something larger than our
>   own desires and wants.
> Help us to reject the fear, self-centredness and distrust of the
>   Levite and priest on the road to Jericho,
> and inspire us to embrace the peace, hope and generosity of
>   spirit of the compassionate Samaritan.
> In Jesus' name,
> Amen

Tuesday

We are family

And the word of the Lord came again to Zechariah: 'This is what the Lord Almighty said: "Administer true justice; show mercy and compassion to one another. Do not oppress the widow or the fatherless, the foreigner or the poor. Do not plot evil against each other."

'But they refused to pay attention; stubbornly they turned their backs and covered their ears. They made their hearts as hard as flint and would not listen to the law or to the words that the Lord Almighty had sent by his Spirit through the earlier prophets.'

ZECHARIAH 7:8–12a

As I sat in my local doctor's surgery recently, a young boy of Middle Eastern origin started staring at me. I smiled at him and said, 'Hello', but he simply kept on staring with inquisitive eyes. Noticing this one-sided conversation, his father nodded his head towards me, smiled and said in a strong accent to his reticent child, 'Come on now, say hello to your uncle.' A smile broke across the hitherto unresponsive little face, and a big, cheerful hello followed.

At first, I was rather taken aback to be called an 'uncle' by a complete stranger. Then I remembered the link between the view of some Middle Eastern cultures that all people are family and their call to care and compassion. After all, the Arabic word for compassion is *rahmah*, and it is found frequently in the Koran. This is similar to the Hebrew word for compassion that our passage today uses (*rachamim*), and both the Arabic and Hebrew are related to words for 'womb'. In other words, both the Muslim scriptures and the Old Testament indicate that our compassion for those around us should reflect family bonds. So compassion is about treating others as if they were our own flesh and blood, as if they had shared the same womb as us.

When I was laid up in bed with a back problem recently, I decided to re-read the Bible from cover to cover. What struck me most about the Old Testament was the many reminders to the Israelites that, as they 'were foreigners in Egypt' (Exodus 22:21), they must show kindness, mercy and generosity to foreigners in their own land, as we see in our passage today. Our faith challenges us to expand our circle of compassion to all, not merely those who are like us or those who happened to have been born in the same country. In recent years there have been discussions in the press, parliament and pulpit about those coming to Europe and those attempting to cross the channel to make a home in our 'green and pleasant land'. Some commentators and politicians have rightly demanded that we see beyond the labels of people as refugees, immigrants or migrants. We are challenged to see them simply as people, just like you and me.

As Christians, we are called to go further than this. This is the profound depth of the challenge of compassion – to see others, not merely as people, not even merely as friends, but as brothers and sisters. The French Cistercian monk Charles de Foucauld referred to this concept as the 'universal brotherhood'. This is a huge challenge to our lives and our politics.

But when we do view others as our family, labels will peel away. The Jesuit priest Anthony de Mello used an analogy of a menu in a restaurant. However much we might salivate while considering the list of food, not one of us will decide to eat the actual menu. It is the food that we want to eat, not the words about the food. As far as possible we must attempt to experience people themselves, rather than experience the labels that we or other people put on them. As soon as we slap a label like 'immigrant' and 'refugee' on a person, our understanding of that individual can become distorted. We start to see the label rather than the person, and every label, of course, has undertones of approval or disapproval.

My wife is German. When I look at her lovingly over a romantic meal, I do not stare into her eyes and say, 'Darling, you are such a beautiful immigrant'! Likewise, in my own church we have individuals from across the globe who are active in the congregation. None of us see them as 'immigrants'. Once we know a person, they cease to be a label and they simply become family.

In light of our faith, then, it makes perfect sense that I was called 'uncle' by that little boy in the doctor's surgery. For Christians, there is no opt-out clause in the Bible's invitation to view others as family. Instead, it lies at the very heart of our faith and is fundamental to our radical call to live out the compassionate kingdom. To affirm Jesus as the Messiah is to say that we will act as he acted – to treat others as our brothers and sisters, whoever they are, whatever their background and however different they might be to us.

Reflection

Find a map of the world – in an atlas, on a globe or on the internet. Take time to slowly and prayerfully look at the countries and either 1) give thanks and pray for God's blessing on people you know, or have known, from the countries that stand out to you or 2) pray for God's blessing on the people from the countries that you know have been through difficulties in recent years – war, civil war, terrorism or natural disasters.

Wednesday

Compassion and wisdom

At Gibeon the Lord appeared to Solomon during the night in a dream, and God said, 'Ask for whatever you want me to give you.'

Solomon answered, 'You have shown great kindness to your servant, my father David, because he was faithful to you and righteous and upright in heart. You have continued this great kindness to him and have given him a son to sit on his throne this very day.

'Now, Lord my God, you have made your servant king in place of my father David. But I am only a little child and do not know how to carry out my duties. Your servant is here among the people you have chosen, a great people, too numerous to count or number. So give your servant a discerning heart to govern your people and to distinguish between right and wrong. For who is able to govern this great people of yours?'

The Lord was pleased that Solomon had asked for this. So God said to him, 'Since you have asked for this and not for long life or wealth for yourself, nor have asked for the death of your enemies but for discernment in administering justice, I will do what you have asked. I will give you a wise and discerning heart, so that there will never have been anyone like you, nor will there ever be. Moreover, I will give you what you have not asked for – both wealth and honour – so that in your lifetime you will have no equal among kings. And if you walk in obedience to me and keep my decrees and commands as David your father did, I will give you a long life.'

1 KINGS 3:5–14

When I was a child, I used to love this story. In a dream, God asks King Solomon, who is new to the throne, to ask for anything he wants. It used to remind me of the genie-in-the-lamp jokes that were popular when I was younger, although I would feel sorry for poor Solomon's one wish – genies in those jokes always offered three! Solomon asks for wisdom. When God commends Solomon's choice, he lists what he could have asked for – long life, wealth and the death of his enemies. In other words, those things that were the typical desires of the kings of the ancient Near East. It is interesting to consider what our own desire might be. What would we choose if we were allowed just one thing? Material goods, popularity, success, long life, good health, promotion or happy relationships? The reality is that Solomon's choice would probably be low on most people's lists. Yet the world would be a much better place if wisdom was at the centre of our thoughts, conversations and actions.

Wisdom is not simply learning or intelligence: 'Knowledge is knowing that a tomato is a fruit, but wisdom is knowing not to put it in a fruit salad', as Brian O'Driscoll, the former Ireland rugby captain, told a confused press conference after one match! Our passage today, though, sheds light on what wisdom really means. Solomon, after all, asks for a 'discerning mind', which is often translated as 'an understanding mind'. The Hebrew here, *lev shome'a*, though, literally means 'a listening heart'. In other words, first, wisdom is linked to both the mind and the heart, and, second, wisdom is to do with discerning, understanding and listening. An important element of wisdom is, therefore, a deep self-awareness and self-understanding of our actions and the impact that they have on others.

By taking a step back from situations and conversations, by working out whether we are acting compassionately, we allow God to hold us and mould us. In the gospels, we are told that people listening to Jesus were 'astonished' and 'amazed' by his wisdom (e.g. Mark 6:2). By embracing self-awareness and welcoming wisdom into our lives, we become more like Jesus. 'I no longer live,' writes the apostle Paul, 'but Christ lives in me' (Galatians 2:20).

Lacking an awareness of ourselves, on the other hand, can lead to us lacking compassion in our lives and in our relationships. Are we aware that the things we say and do to others have a profound effect on them? Do we realise how much we judge people because of how they look, how they act or how different they happen to be from us? Do we recognise that by generalising about certain groups of people, we are contributing to bigotry and hatred, which might ultimately lead to violence, even if we're not involved directly in such actions ourselves?

How we achieve a self-awareness of our attitudes and actions is a challenge to each of us. Prayer is an important step in understanding how we affect the world around us. The 16th-century contemplative Ignatius suggested a prayer practice called the examen, which involves taking time to sit in silence and reflect on how we acted and reacted that day. This can be an immensely powerful and liberating daily practice that can transform thought and action.

The examen is just one way to travel in awareness and wisdom, not least because it helps us recognise both our strengths and our faults. In the Hebrew tradition, when something was named, some power was taken over it – Adam named the animals and Jesus named demons before he demanded that they leave. In recognising and naming our reactions, prejudices, fears, dislikes and temptations, we gradually take back the hold these things have over us. As the theologian Dietrich Bonhoeffer writes, 'Sin wants to remain unknown. It shuns the light. In the darkness of the unexpressed it poisons the whole being of a person.' Through a process of honest self-awareness, we can be liberated to embrace wisdom and so see ourselves and others as God sees us all – broken, but loved unconditionally; hurt, but hopeful; struggling, but fully accepted. As such, this self-examining awareness must not lead to captivity and guilt, but to a wisdom that brings the freedom of a truly compassionate life.

Reflection

Practise the examen this evening. If you like, light a candle to remind yourself of God's presence. Sit in silence and reflect on your day – how you acted, how you reacted. As you review the day, thank God for the gifts you received, but also pay attention to how you might have come across to others. Then leave the day with God, and commit that tomorrow you will actively bring compassion, peace and joy to the lives of others.

Thursday

Compassion for all creatures

Then God said to Noah and to his sons with him: 'I now establish my covenant with you and with your descendants after you and with every living creature that was with you – the birds, the livestock and all the wild animals, all those that came out of the ark with you – every living creature on earth. I establish my covenant with you: never again will all life be destroyed by the waters of a flood; never again will there be a flood to destroy the earth.'

And God said, 'This is the sign of the covenant I am making between me and you and every living creature with you, a covenant for all generations to come: I have set my rainbow in the clouds, and it will be the sign of the covenant between me and the earth. Whenever I bring clouds over the earth and the rainbow appears in the clouds, I will remember my covenant between me and you and all living creatures of every kind. Never again will the waters become a flood to destroy all life. Whenever the rainbow appears in the clouds, I will see it and remember the everlasting covenant between God and all living creatures of every kind on the earth.'

So God said to Noah, 'This is the sign of the covenant I have established between me and all life on the earth.'

GENESIS 9:8–17

When I was growing up, I did not have a pet for any great length of time. I had a rabbit named Twm Twitch for a few years, a guinea pig named Rupert for a few weeks and a newt named Isaac Newton for a few days, before he escaped and was found shrivelled up on the kitchen floor. I enjoyed seeing creatures in the wild, but I wasn't really an animal person. My first job was in a Wimpy burger bar, and I persuaded my first girlfriend to give up her vegetarianism and start eating proper food – quarter-pound Wimpy burgers with that lovely pink relish they used. Unconsciously, animals were, in my mind, expendable and exploitable – they were 'things' given to us by God to be eaten, worn and used for our own purposes, however selfish and self-centred those purposes may be.

At the age of 21, I underwent a Damascene conversion in my attitude to animals. At the root of this transformation was today's passage, and I remember the scales falling from my eyes as I read it. It became clear to me that scripture's ethical demands had far-reaching implications and went beyond simply caring for our own species. After all, the covenant between God and his people in the Old Testament, which then became a covenant between God and us all in the New Testament, is not simply about humankind. One of the most striking aspects of the Noahic covenant is that it is made between God and 'all living creatures of every kind on the earth', including 'the birds, the livestock and all the wild animals'. As if to hammer this home, that fact is mentioned five times in this short passage alone!

With this realisation, my view of Jesus' teaching on love was completely transformed. It suddenly became obvious to me that our call as Christians to compassion and care should not simply include our human brothers and sisters, but should embrace all living things. In the Middle Ages, Francis of Assisi had famously brought this to the attention of fellow Christians in his kindness towards all living creatures and in speaking of 'Brother Sun, Sister Moon'. In the 20th century, the doctor and theologian Albert Schweitzer summed up this concept in the phrase 'reverence for life'. Yet, in so many matters concerning non-human life, we Christians have our faith boxed up. We certainly unpack it and it comes out when we are considering personal morality and social injustices, but other issues, such as animal rights, are seen as secular concerns that are quite distinct from our faith.

Compassion, though, compels us to view each living thing as part of God's kingdom and insists that we ask difficult, but urgent, questions about our environment and the creatures that inhabit God's creation.

Why are animals treated so poorly? What can we do to ensure animals are treated better? How can we personally live out our compassion and love towards the natural world? How should Christians react to mass extinction of species on land and sea? What implications does 'reverence for life' have on the challenge of climate change?

When it comes to such questions, not least with issues of intensive farming, laboratory experiments, live exports and other questions of animal rights, the old adage 'This is the way it's always been' is no longer an acceptable excuse. As Christians, we are challenged to question what we've been taught, to consider the biblical imperative to value our fellow creatures and to view everything in the light of Jesus' compassion. 'Creation itself will be liberated from its bondage to decay and brought into the freedom and glory of the children of God', writes Paul (Romans 8:21).

But our faith is not just about viewing the world in a certain way – it's also about changing the world. We need to live out the gospel, not simply to think and talk about it. Each one of us needs to work out personally how much this call to a wider compassion will impact our everyday lives. We can all certainly take small practical steps towards change: we can pray for all living things, educate ourselves on the issues surrounding animal welfare, read the Bible with the importance of all creation in mind, get involved in campaigns, support animal welfare and environmental charities, be selective in shopping, forgo meat and animal products for one or two days a week, and spread the word by encouraging friends, family and colleagues to themselves read about such issues. Getting our priorities right is certainly the first step, but that means little if we are not then inspired into righteous action.

Reflection

Research some issues around animal welfare and care for the environment by spending some time browsing through the internet pages of animal and environmental charities – some to consider are the WWF, Greenpeace and Christian charities like A Rocha, SARX or the Anglican Society for the Welfare of Animals. Now take some time to pray about some of the issues that you have read about. If you don't have access to the internet, spend time in prayer for all creatures, great and small, and for a transformation of attitudes and actions towards them.

Friday

Compassion's real challenge

Who shall separate us from the love of Christ? Shall trouble or hardship or persecution or famine or nakedness or danger or sword? As it is written:

'For your sake we face death all day long;
we are considered as sheep to be slaughtered.'

No, in all these things we are more than conquerors through him who loved us. For I am convinced that neither death nor life, neither angels nor demons, neither the present nor the future, nor any powers, neither height nor depth, nor anything else in all creation, will be able to separate us from the love of God that is in Christ Jesus our Lord.

ROMANS 8:35–39

As a writer, I had always dreamed of speaking at the wonderful Hay Festival in Wales. One year, I received an email out of the blue – my dream had come true. The email invited me to speak at Hay in the Parc. I sat back and imagined Hay in the Parc taking place in a lush, green park, with everyone sitting around drinking Pimms, eating canapés and enjoying the sunshine as they listened to famous authors reciting prose and poetry. But then I read the rest of the email. The 'Parc' in question was no idyllic, verdant park, but Parc prison, the secure category B jail in south Wales.

Hay in the Parc is a sister literary festival to the main festival in Hay. Its aim is to inspire prisoners (many of whom have reading skills below those of a ten-year-old) to engage further with learning and, ultimately, to change their lives. The festival offers opportunities for prisoners to engage with authors and to attend creative writing classes, and, since it began in 2008, it has touched the lives of over 2,000 prisoners.

My own visit turned out to be quite an experience. Having written a book on suffering, I thought it would be an engaging subject to present to the prisoners. As I sat in the prison chapel beforehand, the chaplain took the opportunity to brief me very generally of the crimes for which the prisoners I would be meeting were being detained. They had not been imprisoned for speeding offences or petty theft, but for crimes that I found completely abhorrent. I began to think about the victims of their crimes. I'm sure that I was echoing the very attitudes that this group of people must face on being released back into our community. Writing about the kingdom of God's call for us to see the face of Christ in everyone we come into contact with is easy; living out the kingdom in our daily lives is much harder. Yet, once the prisoners were in the room, their humanity, humour and humility drew me a little way down the path of seeing them as their loving Father sees them.

The experience also helped me realise the deep pain and suffering so many prisoners have been through, in their childhoods, before their crimes or since their convictions. Our passage today reminds us that God's love is for all who face trials or tribulations. One of the Parc prisoners that I met, let's call him Will, reflected the sense of abandonment, loneliness and alienation that many prisoners feel when he wrote in the collection *Windows: Christian writings from HMP Parc*:

It started like any normal day, but this was the day I died. Yes, I said died. Well, at the time it felt like I had just died. I no longer had a first name, I was given a number and sat in a room that felt so cold and dark, but looking at the clock on the wall it was saying 2.00 pm. But to me time meant nothing. I had just lost my life, my family, everything I own… I would sit on my bed reflecting on who I was and what I had done before coming to prison and how much better it would be to kill myself; this hell would end. I would close my eyes and I was back home with my family and it would be just a normal day, the wife doing wifely things and the kids just being kids. Then I would open my eyes and I was back in this cold cell that I call hell.

In the illustrated edition of Philip Yancey's book *What's So Amazing about Grace?*, there is a page with the words 'The one God loves' and a small square of mirrored paper that allows us to look directly at ourselves. Powerfully, on turning to the next page, the words 'Like me' are printed along with a picture of Timothy McVeigh, the Oklahoma bomber who killed over 160 people. Yes, God loves all the victims of crime, who need our complete support and care. But the radical thing about God's love is that he also loves those in prisons worldwide, and he offers them his peace and compassion. Likewise, he loves the families and friends of prisoners, whose lives are often torn apart.

There are, after all, *no* conditions to God's love. He does not say, 'Change, and then I will love you.' He loves us in the hope that we will want to be transformed. Whatever we do, whatever we think and whoever we are, we are all infinitely loved. This is the most unique and beautiful thing about God's love. But it is also one of the most difficult things to accept.

It is not surprising that most of us find this hugely challenging, especially when we consider heinous crimes and notorious criminals. I certainly do. But the scandal of God's grace is that nothing or no one is beyond his love. That is what makes our own compassion for others so challenging and what makes God's compassion so powerfully transforming. As Will wrote at the end of his contribution in *Windows*:

As I sat in the chapel listening to what was being said something happened to me. I started not to feel alone. This guy who was talking seemed like he was talking to me, even though the room was filled with other prisoners. It felt like he was just telling me a story about a bloke called Jesus. After chapel, I went back to my cell from hell, but this time it felt different. It was the same cell, but it did not feel so cold and I never felt like I was by myself again.

Reflection

Buy a copy of a newspaper today. Look through it and ask yourself who in the news stories upsets you or makes you angry? Be truthful with yourself by considering the kind of people you might find it difficult to show compassion towards. Take time in prayer to ask God to help you see others as he sees them.

Saturday

Us-and-them attitudes

Do not lie to each other, since you have taken off your old self with its practices and have put on the new self, which is being renewed in knowledge in the image of its Creator. Here there is no Gentile or Jew, circumcised or uncircumcised, barbarian, Scythian, slave or free, but Christ is all, and is in all.

Therefore, as God's chosen people, holy and dearly loved, clothe yourselves with compassion, kindness, humility, gentleness and patience. Bear with each other and forgive one another if any of you has a grievance against someone. Forgive as the Lord forgave you. And over all these virtues put on love, which binds them all together in perfect unity.

Let the peace of Christ rule in your hearts, since as members of one body you were called to peace. And be thankful.

COLOSSIANS 3:9–15

When I was in school, as a way to pass the time on the final day of term the teachers always used to revert to the same game – the 'lifeboat game'. It would start with a tale of woe, in which a terrible storm sinks a cruise ship in some remote sea, leaving only ten survivors. Unfortunately, they are all packed on a tiny lifeboat which can only carry eight. So, the question is posed – which are the two poor souls that, to be blunt, have to be thrown overboard? Who was worth saving? Who was expendable?

I was reminded of that game by a recent comment left on a blog post I had written about compassion for refugees. 'Your talk of compassion is a lovely sentiment, but it's one that we certainly can't afford,' the contributor wrote before bringing up the lifeboat analogy. This attitude reflects something that generations have been brought up believing – that some lives are worth more than others. And, of course, more often than not we don't consider ourselves, our friends and our families as the expendable ones.

Changing a way of thinking that has been instilled in us since childhood is no easy feat. This lifeboat attitude is so woven into the fabric of our society that it is difficult to even be aware of it in our own thinking. Many of our newspapers reinforce this attitude in our minds, suggesting that in every moral or social decision we are making a choice between 'us' and 'them'. And so, both individuals and groups of people are stigmatised because they might be different from us in some way – whether in race, gender, culture, sexuality, nationality, religion or socioeconomic status.

But our faith makes it clear to us that there is no 'choice' that we have to make. Compassion brings us to recognise that there is no 'us and them' – that we are *all* children of God, loved and unique. Our passage today echoes this fact and shows that first-century Palestine was not immune to dividing people into groups of 'us' and 'them'. As Jesus had done in parables such as the prodigal son and the good Samaritan, Paul also challenges the status quo. 'Here,' he wrote in today's passage, 'there is no Gentile or Jew, circumcised or uncircumcised, barbarian, Scythian, slave or free, but Christ is all, and is in all.' In recent times, we have faced, and indeed continue to face, so many challenges and difficulties – climate change, racism, pandemics, terrorism, crime and political upheaval. Our faith helps us to accept the simple fact that we are all in this together.

The call of a Christian, then, is not to get but to give, not to be self-centred but to serve. As such, this call combats the us-and-them virus that continues to infect our society today. By recognising each person as an individual worthy of respect, compassion and equality, we are inspired to reject the marginalisation of the vulnerable, the neglect of the disabled and the elderly, the stigmatisation of the poor and the increasing hate crimes against different races and religions in our society.

A former student of mine, Revd Dr Keith Hebden, lives out his Christian call in a very practical way. National newspapers have reported on his arrest for speaking out against drone warfare, his visit to the hundreds of migrants living in appalling conditions in Calais, and his 40-day fast to draw attention to the rise in poverty in Britain. We may not ourselves take such dramatic steps in living out our Christian life, but each and every one of us can raise our voices and speak up for those who are continually on the other side of the us-and-them equation in our society. Silence must never be an option when we face hatred and oppression. As Keith Hebden wrote, adapting Nazi concentration camp survivor Martin Niemöller's words:

> First they came for disabled people, but I did not speak up because I am not disabled. Then they came for the unemployed, but I did not speak up and risk my own job. Then they came for the unions, but maybe we don't need unions anymore. Then they came for migrants, but my middle-class guilt meant I kept my head down. Finally, they came for me and there was no one left to speak out for me.

Reflection

Consider who are the 'others' in our world today – those people who are often stigmatised and who our society sometimes treats as expendable. Pray that we are never afraid to speak out against those who attempt to marginalise, blame or belittle both individuals and groups of people.

=== **HOLY WEEK** ===

Open our pain
to your peace

Palm Sunday

From adoration to agony to glory

As they approached Jerusalem and came to Bethphage and Bethany at the Mount of Olives, Jesus sent two of his disciples, saying to them, 'Go to the village ahead of you, and just as you enter it, you will find a colt tied there, which no one has ever ridden. Untie it and bring it here. If anyone asks you, "Why are you doing this?" say, "The Lord needs it and will send it back here shortly."'

They went and found a colt outside in the street, tied at a doorway. As they untied it, some people standing there asked, 'What are you doing, untying that colt?' They answered as Jesus had told them to, and the people let them go. When they brought the colt to Jesus and threw their cloaks over it, he sat on it. Many people spread their cloaks on the road, while others spread branches they had cut in the fields. Those who went ahead and those who followed shouted,

'Hosanna!'

'Blessed is he who comes in the name of the Lord!'

'Blessed is the coming kingdom of our father David!'

'Hosanna in the highest heaven!'

MARK 11:1–10

In our passage today, Jesus begins his journey of transformation. Here, in the triumphal entry into Jerusalem, he is worshipped and praised by the crowds on the roadside, giving us a foretaste of his future glory. Before the glorious resurrection, though, he will be beaten, tortured and crucified. The journey of Holy Week is, therefore, a journey of transformation from adoration to agony to glory.

The word in Greek for 'transformation' is *metamorphoomai*, which is related to our English word 'metamorphosis'. Mark's gospel uses this word shortly before this triumphal entry, when Jesus was transfigured on a high mountain. The only other times the word is used in the New Testament, though, is in reference to transformation in our own lives. Paul uses the word twice – in Romans and in 2 Corinthians. It is clear that we all go through events and circumstances, sometimes painful and sometimes joyful, which change the ways we think and act. Paul, though, suggests that we are not subject to blind fate in this change. With God's help, we can slowly be transformed into Jesus' likeness. Such a transformation has huge implications – on the way we view things, the way we use our time and money and the way we treat others and the world around us.

In the triumphal entry, the people praising Jesus refer to 'the coming kingdom'. God's kingdom is all about the power of transformation. This life-giving and life-affirming change starts in our hearts, but quickly permeates our everyday lives, as we grow more and more to reflect Jesus and we help to usher in his kingdom.

The philosopher Loren Eiseley tells a story about an old man who is walking along the shore after a big storm and the beach is littered with starfish as far as the eye can see. In the distance, the man notices a small boy approaching. As the boy walks, he pauses every so often and then bends down to pick up a starfish and throw it back into the sea. 'Good morning,' the man calls out. 'Can I ask what you are doing?' The young boy replies, 'The tide has washed these starfish up on to the beach, and they can't return to the sea by themselves; when the sun gets high, they'll die, unless I throw them back into the water.' The old man replies, 'But there are thousands of starfish on this beach; you won't really be able to make much of a difference.' The boy bends down again, picks up yet another starfish and throws it back into the ocean. Then he turns and says, 'It made a difference to that one!'

This tale holds a truth about God's kingdom. In every little act of kindness, love or forgiveness, we are taking a leap of faith as to the difference we make. We take that leap in the reassuring knowledge that our fellow Christians are also on this journey of transformation.

After all, in a loaf of bread, there are many grains that are ground and kneaded together, but once that loaf has been baked, the individual grains cannot be identified. We are left with one loaf which serves one purpose – to feed and nourish. By ourselves we are grains of wheat, but together we are the bread of life, the body of Christ. So, our everyday, seemingly insignificant, loving actions build up to a critical mass.

In this way, our small compassionate actions can make an immense difference in our communities. Researchers at the University of Sheffield recently compared censuses of the past 40 years and discovered that communities are far less rooted than they once were – more people live alone, people move houses more often and membership of social groups, such as Rotary clubs, Scouts and Guides, has halved in recent years. This, of course, is before we even mention the decline in church membership. The result is, in the words of Danny Dorling, 'even the weakest community in 1971 was stronger than any community now'.

Today's communities, then, need a new vision of what the future holds for our children and grandchildren. The body of Christ, the people of change and glorious transformation, can gift our communities with a glorious hope. The Mexican wave is always initiated by a small group of people standing up and sitting down. The wave quickly spreads all the way around a stadium and finishes with many thousands involved. The world of the 21st century is an interconnected one. The rapid spread of the vicious Covid-19 virus is testament to that fact. But this interconnection also has many positives. Just like a Mexican wave, the actions of a small group of individuals can affect the whole system very quickly. 'Be the change you want to see' is a slogan in the environmental movement, but this idea is also at very heart of the transformative message of our faith.

Reflection

Close your eyes and picture the scene of the triumphal entry – so much joy and excitement. Now picture the crucifixion with its deep grief, sadness and pain. Finally, picture the resurrected Jesus – glorious and triumphant. This was Jesus' transformation, his metamorphoomai. Now take some time to prayerfully sit in Jesus' presence, asking him to change you into his likeness. This will be your own transformation, your own metamorphoomai. By contemplating Jesus and spending time with him, we become the change we want to see and become part of that beautiful and complete transformation that his kingdom brings to individuals, relationships and communities.

Holy Monday

The storms of life

There is a time for everything,
   and a season for every activity under the heavens:
   a time to be born and a time to die,
   a time to plant and a time to uproot,
   a time to kill and a time to heal,
   a time to tear down and a time to build,
   a time to weep and a time to laugh,
   a time to mourn and a time to dance,
   a time to scatter stones and a time to gather them,
   a time to embrace and a time to refrain from embracing,
   a time to search and a time to give up,
   a time to keep and a time to throw away,
   a time to tear and a time to mend,
   a time to be silent and a time to speak,
   a time to love and a time to hate,
   a time for war and a time for peace.
ECCLESIASTES 3:1–8

Only a day after I finished the Pilgrim's Way across north Wales, having walked almost 140 miles, I felt a painful twinge in my back. In the following few weeks, the pain got increasingly worse and I had to endure numerous medical appointments and scans. Accompanying the physical pain was the mental angst. Worries about the future tore me away from the present. They were invariably worse in the dead of night, when I had no distractions to keep negative thoughts polluting my mind.

We live in a society that attempts, as best it can, to avoid pain and suffering. Sometimes, though, the storms of life are inescapable. When I was recovering from my back injury, a friend rather cryptically said to me, 'You need to face your pain like the great bear hunt.' It was only when my youngest son chose *We're Going on a Bear Hunt* as his bedtime story a few nights later that I understood something of what she meant. In this classic children's book, written by former children's laureate Michael Rosen, a family searches for a bear by facing various challenging terrains – forest, mud, long grass and snow. With each different environment, we are told that 'we can't go over it; we can't go under it; oh no, we have to go through it!'

As many of us have found in the Covid-19 pandemic, which is still prevalent as I write this, sometimes we have to face the reality that our times of pain, hurt or grief are unavoidable. At those times, we have to 'gird up our loins', as the Bible puts it (see, for example, the NRSV translation of 1 Kings 18:46 and the footnote to 1 Peter 1:13) and face the misery of suffering head on. We cannot be like rugby players, skilfully sidestepping opponents; instead, we are forced to be like American football players, confronting opposite numbers head-on by crashing into them.

When I was growing up, today's passage always confused me. I loved its poetic prose, not least when I was listening to The Byrds' US number 1 hit song 'Turn! Turn! Turn!', which adapts these beautiful words. My confusion, though, was rooted in the fact that, in its catalogue of paired polarities, the passage implied that 'war', 'slaying' and 'hate' were unavoidable in our lives. Now I realise the writer of Ecclesiastes was not making a point about ethical or social matters, but was using a popular rabbinic literary technique to present a wisdom about the transience of events, emotions and activities.

On my long pilgrimage along the coastline of north Wales, I spent many hours gazing out at the Irish Sea as I rested with my lunch or my trusty flask of tea. During that walk, I was struck by how quickly the sea could be transformed, sometimes slowly from day-to-day, but other times in a matter of hours. When a child draws the sea, they will immediately reach for the blue crayon. By spending a length of time staring out to the changeable sea, though, a plethora of beautiful colours emerge. These are often related to the sea's condition – sometimes threatening and disturbingly dark; on other occasions calm and crystal clear. One day, as I sat on a rock on the edge of a clifftop, I wrote in my notepad that the waves were like rolling, unforgiving white juggernauts crashing against the headland. The very next day, by now on a sandy beach, I jotted down that the sea was a serene stillness gently caressing the golden shoreline.

Like the sea, our life journey is ever-changing. Sometimes all seems tranquil – we are blessed with times of joy, pleasure or celebration. But sometimes storms rage around us – we have to face times of pain, anxiety or grief. 'There is a time for everything,' as our passage puts it, 'and a season for every activity under the heavens.' At those seasons of suffering in my own life, it has helped me to remind myself that, like the rolling waves of the tide, our lives have a natural ebb and flow. Life is not a straight line, from birth to death, emerging from darkness and returning to darkness, or, indeed, from light to light. Rather, as the writer of Ecclesiastes had noticed, life is cyclical. The winters of our suffering can certainly be dark, long, cold and painful, but spring will burst forth. We wait for the snowdrops, because we know the daffodils will soon follow. We trust the nature of the seasons that this will happen, just as we who are Christians learn to trust that God will lead us out of our wait, however long and painful. The sixth-century theologian Boethius describes life as a wheel: 'We rise up on the spokes but we're soon cast back down into the depths. Good times pass away, but then so do the bad. Change is our tragedy, but it's also our hope. The worst of times, like the best, are always passing away.'

This way of viewing life can gradually transform our anxious thoughts by giving us the strength to notice and value those little signs of spring breaking through the harshness of winter – to notice and value those daily moments of joy and grace that emerge despite our continuing pain and frustration. This is as powerful a healing as any physical cure could offer. As an old proverb puts it, 'Sometimes God calms the storm, but sometimes God calms the sailor.'

Reflection

A prayer to be prayed slowly and mindfully – allow each word and phrase to inspire your walk with God:

Lord of peace,
we bring to you our past – both our seasons of joy and our seasons
 of difficulty or sadness,
help us to recognise your support, comfort and presence during
 those times, even at moments when you may have felt distant,
and, whatever we might be facing now, we ask you help us notice
 your light illuminating the path of our journeys.
In Jesus' name,
Amen

Holy Tuesday

Wilderness times

The desert and the parched land will be glad;
　the wilderness will rejoice and blossom.
Like the crocus, it will burst into bloom;
　it will rejoice greatly and shout for joy.
The glory of Lebanon will be given to it,
　the splendour of Carmel and Sharon;
they will see the glory of the Lord,
　the splendour of our God.
Strengthen the feeble hands,
　steady the knees that give way;
say to those with fearful hearts,
　'Be strong, do not fear;
your God will come,
　he will come with vengeance;
with divine retribution
　he will come to save you.'
Then will the eyes of the blind be opened
　and the ears of the deaf unstopped.
Then will the lame leap like a deer,
　and the mute tongue shout for joy.
Water will gush forth in the wilderness
　and streams in the desert.
The burning sand will become a pool,
　the thirsty ground bubbling springs.
In the haunts where jackals once lay,
　grass and reeds and papyrus will grow.
And a highway will be there;
　it will be called the Way of Holiness;
　it will be for those who walk on that Way.

ISAIAH 35:1–8a

Apart from a brief visit to New Mexico and a love of the 1962 film about a fellow Welshman, *Lawrence of Arabia*, my experience of deserts has been limited. The early Israelites, though, would have been familiar with desert life. Much of the Middle East is, after all, barren wilderness. As such, they would have known the great challenges of spending time in the desert – the scorching sun, the burning sand, the agonising thirst, the unbearable hunger, the extreme cold at night and the bleak loneliness. They would have also had ample experience of the lush exceptions to the desert all around them – not only oases of foliage and water, but also large areas of fertile, green land, like the Jordan valley and the region around the Sea of Galilee.

Isaiah was an advisor to the king of Judah in the eighth century BC when he wrote today's passage. Within his own country, he was witnessing oppression and injustice, while there was also the real threat of violence from enemies encircling them, not least from Assyria. It was a time of great pain and suffering in both Israel and Judah. It is no surprise, then, that he compares their predicament to a harsh and unforgiving wilderness. In this passage, though, he reassures his fellow citizens that this time in the desert is only temporary – God promises renewal, new life and living water.

In the Bible, it is not only Israel itself that faces times in the wilderness. In fact, every major character goes through some sort of desert experience. Sometimes they go through quite literal wilderness experiences, with, for example, Abraham, Moses and Jesus all spending time in the barren land of the Middle East. For most biblical characters, though, the wilderness experience is not literal but takes a more dramatic form, like Jonah in the whale and Paul's blindness. The author Joseph Campbell, in his work on the myth of the hero, notes that other cultures record the same journey taken by characters who are forced to leave behind security and domesticity to undergo a turbulent desert experience. We see the same step into turmoil and testing in our modern myths – from Luke Skywalker in *Star Wars* (1977) to Katniss Everdeen in *The Hunger Games* (2012).

In reality, of course, all of us have these periods in the wilderness. Some may actually choose to undertake these difficult journeys into uncertainty and challenge. For example, Ignatius of Loyola, founder of the Jesuits, lived in a cave for a year, not cutting his hair and wearing only rags. Most of us, though, have little choice as to our desert moments. They are thrust upon us in our turbulent lives, whether through illness, injury, grief, loss or relationship difficulties. We are unable to avoid being thrown into these desert journeys that are invariably lonely, painful and frustrating. It is at these times that Isaiah's words give us hope and peace. After all, they not only remind us that our desert moments are temporary and that God promises a fullness of revival and restoration, but also that, even in the wilderness, God is still working and his kingdom can break through at our most unhappy times. As theologian Joan Chittister put it, 'There is a light in us that only darkness itself can illuminate.'

In other words, although the desert is dry, lonely and painful, it offers its own opportunities and answers, especially if we hold on to God's promise that light is around the corner, however long that corner may be. So, in our deserts, many of us learn dependence, resilience and determination, as we call upon strength we didn't realise we had. Furthermore, calamity, as disruptive as it is, often allows an opportunity for space, reflection and, ultimately, for growth and enlightenment. All these signs of life point to God's kingdom being powerfully present, even at times of despair, darkness and pain. 'There is no waste in the wasteland,' as church leader Mike Pilavachi puts it.

And so God meets us in those moments of our lives when he seems most distant. In fact, stripped bare and finding ourselves in an inhospitable wilderness, we are sometimes left with nothing but him. At those painful moments in our lives, we are forced to relinquish control to him and open ourselves to his kingdom. After all, his light is all the more dazzling in a dark place, his water more refreshing in the desert and his peace more comforting in our pain.

Reflection

A prayer to be prayed slowly and mindfully – allow each word and phrase to inspire your walk with God:

> *Loving God,*
> *when facing the frustration, loneliness and darkness of the*
>   *wilderness, help us to open our lives to your kingdom,*
> *pour your living water on us that we may be refreshed,*
> *feed us your life-giving bread that we are assured of your*
>   *presence,*
> *shine your light on us that we may see your glory.*
> *In Jesus' name,*
> *Amen*

Holy Wednesday

At the name of Jesus

Now it was the governor's custom at the festival to release a prisoner chosen by the crowd. At that time they had a well-known prisoner whose name was Jesus Barabbas. So when the crowd had gathered, Pilate asked them, 'Which one do you want me to release to you: Jesus Barabbas, or Jesus who is called the Messiah?' For he knew it was out of self-interest that they had handed Jesus over to him.

While Pilate was sitting on the judge's seat, his wife sent him this message: 'Don't have anything to do with that inno-cent man, for I have suffered a great deal today in a dream because of him.'

But the chief priests and the elders persuaded the crowd to ask for Barabbas and to have Jesus executed.

'Which of the two do you want me to release to you?' asked the governor.

'Barabbas,' they answered.

'What shall I do, then, with Jesus who is called the Messiah?' Pilate asked.

They all answered, 'Crucify him!'

'Why? What crime has he committed?' asked Pilate.

But they shouted all the louder, 'Crucify him!'

MATTHEW 27:15–23

For people in the ancient world, a person's name said something essential about them. Even today, we forget how important our names are to us. In Welsh, we rarely, if ever, introduce ourselves by saying 'My name is Trystan'. Rather, we say 'I am Trystan' (*Trystan 'dwi*). In other words, our names are absolutely integral to who we are – they define us to our core. I made a video some time back in which we asked people, 'Who are you?' In almost all the interviews, the first answer was their name. Only when prompted did they flesh out their answer with, 'I'm a mother', 'I'm a lawyer', 'I'm a rugby supporter' and so on.

Scientists have even shown that a child's name has a major impact on their life. Research is being carried out to find out why there are a hugely disproportionate number of certain names, like Eleanor, Catherine and Peter, at Oxford University. There are also numerous studies into nominative determinism, researching why people are often drawn to trades and professions that relate to their surnames – why there are higher percentages of cooks with the surname Baker, of ministers of religion with the surnames Bishop and Parsons, and so on. (Then, we have the world-record-breaking sprinter Usain Bolt, a famous Chinese-American lawyer called Sue Yoo and two prominent urologists called D. Weedon and A.J. Splatt!)

In the ancient world, it was a common belief that a name could express a person's destiny. In the Jewish tradition especially, a person's name was not just a label. Rather, a name said something profound about that person, so much so that people even changed their names if they went through a life-changing event. For the early Israelites, a name reflected a character and identity – through your name, the world would know something about who you were, what you did and where your life was heading.

The name Jesus was popular among first-century Israelites. It is a form of Joshua, meaning 'God saves'. The early church father Origen was so troubled by the fact that today's passage gives Barabbas the forename Jesus that he suggested that it must have been added by a heretic who had cunningly adapted the gospel. Although 'Barabbas' is now a colloquial slur in various languages (such as Spanish, Serbian and Croatian) for a bad person or rogue, many have suggested that Barabbas' crime may simply have been a desire to free the Jewish people from their Roman oppressors. In the blockbuster film *King of Kings* (1961), for example, Barabbas is depicted as a friend of Judas Iscariot, with both being aligned to the Zealots, a Jewish political group determined to bring down their Roman oppressors. Likewise, the later animated film *The Miracle Maker* (1999) also presents Barabbas as a Jewish insurgent, determined to save Israel from Roman captivity.

So it makes sense that Barabbas' name was Jesus – he was also interested in saving people. The salvation offered by Jesus of Nazareth, though, is very different from that promised by the firstcentury Jewish Zealots. The angel in the Christmas story informs Joseph that his son is to be named Jesus because he 'will save his people from their sins' (Matthew 1:21). Very different from Barabbas' promise of redemption through power and violence, Jesus' salvation deals with our worries, anxieties and destructive patterns of thinking and behaviour. He brings a peace that the world cannot give (John 14:27).

In this sense, Jesus' salvation is very much related to conquering fear. The angels in the birth narratives of both Luke and Matthew not only announce the importance of Jesus' name, but they also reassure Mary and Joseph that there is no need to be afraid. Fear can keep us trapped and incarcerated, which can lead to anxiety, sadness and even isolation. Salvation, though, brings freedom from the enslavement of such temptations or worries. It brings peace to our pain and suffering. It brings hope to those of us who sometimes feel lonely, sad or misunderstood. Yes, that was part of the message of Christmas, but it is also very much part of the message of Holy Week – a week that guarantees us that the rejected, tortured and crucified Jesus stands alongside us in these struggles.

Reflection

Take some time to consider your own difficulties and struggles. You may be inclined towards worry, depression, a particular temptation, anxiety or anger or you might have times of loneliness or sadness. Take heart in the fact that Jesus knows what suffering is and that his salvation ensures our struggles can be redeemed. In a time of silence and prayer, ask God to bring you something of his peace that passes all understanding.

Maundy Thursday

Kenosis

In your relationships with one another, have the same mindset
as Christ Jesus:

who, being in very nature God,
    did not consider equality with God something to be used
      to his own advantage;
rather, he made himself nothing
    by taking the very nature of a servant,
    being made in human likeness.
And being found in appearance as a man,
    he humbled himself
    by becoming obedient to death –
    even death on a cross!
Therefore God exalted him to the highest place
    and gave him the name that is above every name,
that at the name of Jesus every knee should bow,
    in heaven and on earth and under the earth,
and every tongue acknowledge that Jesus Christ is Lord,
    to the glory of God the Father.

PHILIPPIANS 2:5–11

One year I spent Maundy Thursday in a freezing cold church in the
village of Llanfairfechan in north Wales. We were informed at the
outset that this was to be a traditional service, which included washing
the feet of twelve members of the congregation who would represent
the twelve disciples. At this point I usually hide behind a pillar, so as
not to volunteer myself accidentally. But I looked around and noticed
that there were only twelve members of the congregation – I had no
escape. Furthermore, the vicar admitted that she had a serious phobia
of feet, so we were to forgive her for wincing as she forced herself to

wash the feet of each and every one of us. It was like someone with a snake phobia forcing themselves to touch snakes. What I thought would have been painful to watch (comical even) was, in fact, an amazingly powerful experience. Here was this minister, emptying herself of pride, humbling herself, as she washed our feet.

As I reflected on this service, it brought to mind today's passage. In particular, when Jesus is said to have 'made himself nothing by taking the very nature of a servant'. The Greek word *kenosis*, here translated as 'made himself nothing', can also be translated as 'emptied himself'. Although only used five times in the New Testament, it is a hugely significant concept, describing how Jesus emptied himself of importance, power and glory. Our passage refers to Jesus becoming a servant, but the Greek word could also be translated as 'slave'. In other words, God allowed himself to be reduced to a slave – a person of no status at all. Although the word *kenosis* is not used in the narrative of Jesus washing his disciples' feet, his selfless action reflects this passage. It was, after all, a powerful symbol of his powerless servanthood.

The philosopher Simone Weil wrote about a time when she helped her parents move house. She noticed that her brother was struggling with a far heavier box than hers. 'Feeling' the struggle that her poor brother was undergoing, she put her own load on to the floor, sat on it and refused to help any further until she was given a similarly heavy box. This heart for service was reflected throughout her life, which was cut short in 1942, at the age of 34, partly as a result of an act of solidarity for her suffering compatriots. Although she was herself already very ill with tuberculosis, she had rationed her food intake to what she believed the Jews in occupied France were being allowed to eat. 'As for her death,' wrote her biographer Richard Rees, 'whatever explanation one may give of it will amount in the end to saying that she died of love.'

Such an extreme empathy as Simone Weil felt towards the world is unusual. However, her desire to serve others and her depth of feeling for the pain of others, crazy as they may seem, are at the very heart of *kenosis*. Jesus lived a life of a slave, so that others may be free; he died the death of a criminal, so that others might live. It goes completely against our logic to be freed by someone who is imprisoned or to get directions from someone who is lost. But logic does not limit *kenosis*. As Karl Barth put it, Jesus moves from 'the heights to the depth, from victory to defeat, from riches to poverty, from triumph to suffering, from life to death'. By doing so, he brings to others those very things that he had moved away from himself. Like Jesus himself, we also need to become slaves, so that we can liberate our fellow slaves.

Kenosis demands that we sacrifice our selfish, separate selves and be reborn again as more selfless, servant souls, going above and beyond our basic care for those around us. This is something of what the apostle Paul meant when he exhorted us to die to our sinful self (Romans 6:11). And this can be done in very practical ways, as we consciously use our resources, whether time or money, to make a difference in the world. We can live out *kenosis* to the people around us – our families, friends, work colleagues or even strangers with whom we come into contact. We can proactively place ourselves in situations where people are suffering or struggling – through our church, charities, hospices or hospitals. We can extend Jesus' unlimited love to the wider world, either by joining movements for social and environmental change or by undertaking acts of compassion for our local communities or for the countryside around us. In all these things, we can live out the sacrificial service of *kenosis*, standing alongside those who are in need and offering Christ to the world with open arms and open hearts.

Reflection

Commit yourself to carrying out an act of servanthood in the next 24 hours – this could be a kind and thoughtful act to help a friend or neighbour, donating money to a charity, helping clear litter in your local community or any act of service that could assist someone.

Good Friday

Facing Golgotha

Then Jesus went with his disciples to a place called Geth-semane, and he said to them, 'Sit here while I go over there and pray.' He took Peter and the two sons of Zebedee along with him, and he began to be sorrowful and troubled. Then he said to them, 'My soul is overwhelmed with sorrow to the point of death. Stay here and keep watch with me.'

Going a little farther, he fell with his face to the ground and prayed, 'My Father, if it is possible, may this cup be taken from me. Yet not as I will, but as you will.'

Then he returned to his disciples and found them sleeping. 'Couldn't you men keep watch with me for one hour?' he asked Peter. 'Watch and pray so that you will not fall into temptation. The spirit is willing, but the flesh is weak.'

He went away a second time and prayed, 'My Father, if it is not possible for this cup to be taken away unless I drink it, may your will be done.'

When he came back, he again found them sleeping, because their eyes were heavy. So he left them and went away once more and prayed the third time, saying the same thing.

Then he returned to the disciples and said to them, 'Are you still sleeping and resting? Look, the hour has come, and the Son of Man is delivered into the hands of sinners.'

MATTHEW 26:36–45

There is a story about a woman in America whose husband was in hospital. He was very ill, and she had been going backwards and for-wards to the hospital for many months. In the end, seeing her husband suffering so badly just all got too much. It was a Christian hospital, and it had a large crucifix outside in the courtyard. So she stormed out to this crucifix and started picking up stones and big clumps of mud and throwing them in anger at the statue of Jesus. The security guards went to stop her, but the chaplain held them back. 'Don't stop her,' he said. 'She's praying.'

In the gospel stories, we learn about prayer through the person of Jesus. We see him going to find quiet places to pray, and he also teaches an actual form of words to pray. But during Holy Week we are reminded that Jesus himself came from a Jewish tradition that had a wide and all-encompassing view of prayer. The Jewish people approached God however they were feeling, good or bad, happy or sad. We see this in a stark way in our passage today.

At Gethsemane, after his last supper, Jesus pleaded with God for a change to the divine plan, that the cup of suffering would be taken away from him. This was a prayer of fear and desperation in which he asks to be saved from the imminent and appalling suffering. But as theologian Dorothee Soelle puts it:

> To this plea Jesus receives no answer; God is silent, as he has been so often in the history of mankind, and Jesus remains alone with his repeated cry, his fear of death, his insane hope, his threatened life.

That silence, as Soelle notes, echoes what many of us feel at certain times in our lives – sometimes God seems distant and, when we go through times of deep grief or trauma, he can even seem absent. Not long after Holy Week in 2020, with the country in a pandemic lockdown, one of my church members tragically lost her youngest sister to Covid-19. In tears, she told me that she had been taken back to the first Holy Week and could relate, more than ever, to the continuation of Jesus' prayer of anguish and abandonment on the cross, when he quoted those words from Psalm 22: 'My God, my God, why have you forsaken me?' (Matthew 27:46).

Both in Gethsemane and later on the cross, Jesus refers to God as 'Father', indicating an intimate and loving relationship that allows him to approach him with his deepest thoughts, feelings and concerns. That relationship with the divine is not exclusive to Jesus – he also offers us that closeness with God and this gives us the assurance that it is okay to approach him with our prayers of protest and pain. If we embrace that intimate relationship with our Father God, nothing is too trivial or too important and nothing is too painful or too secular to talk to him about. A father–child relationship allows us to lay bare all our experiences and emotions before God – our joys, pain, despair, questioning and cries for help. 'The best prayers,' wrote John Bunyan, 'have often more groans than words.' Because of those very groans, there is even room for protest, as shown in the Old Testament, especially in the books of Job and the Psalms.

Sometimes, we feel like throwing clumps of mud and stones at God. The ancient religions that were around when our faith was in its early days would have seen that as offensive and blasphemous. But our faith is a strange path to take – it's a faith where the weakest are glorified, the powerful are toppled, a servant is enthroned with a crown made of thorns and a God allows himself to be murdered in a terrifying and bloody way. And this strange Christian faith tells us that it's necessary to take *all* our feelings to God, not just the happy ones and not just the sad ones, but also our feelings of frustration, pain, anger, hurt, disbelief, doubt, scepticism, disappointment and dissatisfaction.

God can take stones and clumps of mud being thrown at him. After all, because of Maundy Thursday and Good Friday, because of the last supper, Gethsemane, Golgotha and the cross, he knows how we're feeling. And, when we cry out to him in times of grief, pain and suffering, we know that his tears are mingling with our own. As theologian Gordon Mursell puts it:

> Our prayer becomes his prayer, our cries of protest his, a gratuitous and useless suffering his as well; and whenever any creature, in gas chambers or hospitals or earthquake-stricken cities, or even in the steel stalls of veal calf pens, cries out in protest at

the sick brutality or sheer grinding unfairness of what they experience, Christ prays in and for them, not dispensing the answers but sharing the questions, and making of their suffering God's own summons to a better and more just world.

Reflection

Find a peaceful place to sit and quieten your mind. Now picture yourself at the foot of a hill in a dry dusty land. It's warm, but it's not sunny. In fact, you notice dark clouds above. Towards the top of the hill, you see three crosses. You start to walk up the hill, passing people as you go. There's a real sense of sadness among the people gathered here, and they are looking up to the cross in the middle. You arrive at the foot of Jesus' cross. From the cross, Jesus looks directly at you. In the words of Teresa of Ávila, 'notice him looking at you' ('mira que te mira'). He is looking at you lovingly. He is not someone harsh or demanding. He does not expect perfection. He understands your doubts, protests, anger, disappointments and frustrations. Give those over to him and simply accept his love. Now, in a time of quiet, just sit in the presence of your creator, who accepts and loves you completely. Allow yourself to be loved.

Holy Saturday

Scarred steel angels

My God, my God, why have you forsaken me?
 Why are you so far from saving me,
 so far from my cries of anguish?
My God, I cry out by day, but you do not answer,
 by night, but I find no rest.
Yet you are enthroned as the Holy One;
 you are the one Israel praises.
In you our ancestors put their trust;
 they trusted and you delivered them.
To you they cried out and were saved;
 in you they trusted and were not put to shame.
But I am a worm and not a man,
 scorned by everyone, despised by the people.
All who see me mock me;
 they hurl insults, shaking their heads.
'He trusts in the Lord,' they say,
 'let the Lord rescue him.
Let him deliver him,
 since he delights in him.'
Yet you brought me out of the womb;
 you made me trust in you, even at my mother's breast.
From birth I was cast on you;
 from my mother's womb you have been my God.
Do not be far from me,
 for trouble is near
 and there is no one to help.

PSALM 22:1–11

The *Angel of the North* is a famous steel sculpture by the side of the A1 road in the north of England. Standing at 20 metres tall, it is an imposing and impressive structure, the height of a five-storey building, which makes it the largest angel sculpture in the world. The theologian Magdalen Smith suggests that Christians should see themselves as steel angels – 'angels', because we live lives of love and compassion, and 'steel', because our faith helps us to stand firm amid life's ups and downs. Interestingly, the sculptor of the *Angel of the North*, Antony Gormley, said he embarked on the project as 'a focus of hope at a painful time of transition for the people of the north-east'. Being steel angels shows that, even at the most dark and difficult times in our lives, we Christians are people of hope.

If others were able to look into each one of our minds and peer into our experiences, they would see that all of us have had moments of great joy (children, grandchildren, parties or uplifting holidays), but they would also see our times of great sadness (grief over the loss of loved ones, illness, disappointment, depression, broken relationships or anxiety and worry). Each of us has had Good Friday and Holy Saturday times in our lives. We are, though, anchored by the hope given to us by our faith. The *Angel of the North* has to withstand storms and winds – winds of over 100 mph beat against this great structure. It bends and sways, but it doesn't break, because its roots are deep and its foundations are strong – 600 tonnes of concrete anchor it to rock 21 metres below ground. In the same way, we cope with our difficult times by being anchored to our faith. We may all experience our Holy Weeks, but, strangely, our roots are in the future – in Easter Sunday and in the knowledge that our God is a God of hope and resurrection.

We are, though, different from a solid steel structure in one important aspect. My eldest son and I love watching superhero films and TV series. We avidly follow the likes of Batman, Spider-Man, Incredible Hulk and Thor. One lesser-known superhero from the Marvel Universe that we enjoy watching is Luke Cage. His rather unusual superpower is unbreakable skin. In other words, his skin cannot be pierced or marked. In my local cathedral in Llandaff, Cardiff, there is a huge figure of the resurrected Christ that hangs above the nave on a concrete arch. It is an inspiring and impressive structure, but, in my view, Jacob Epstein's masterpiece has one flaw – Jesus has no wounds on his hands and feet. It is as if Jesus is like the superhero Luke Cage, unpierced and unmarked. Yet for the resurrection to offer us the hope for healing, the Bible tells us that Jesus' body *was* scarred by sin and violence; his wounds were not hidden away, and yet he rose again and lived.

All of us have, at times, been hurt and scarred by people and events – people have said things to us that have cut us deeply, things have happened to us that have left us hurt and wounded, and grief and loss have left aching holes in our lives. All of us have, therefore, felt the pain and abandonment of today's passage from the Psalms, which Jesus himself quotes on the cross. Through the presence of such protest in the pages of the Bible, and on Jesus' lips on the cross, we are reassured that God is listening to our cries of anguish and loss and, if we allow him, he will use our painful experiences after he brings us through the other side, healed and hopeful. After all, our scars, physical and emotional, are the things that make us who we are and we must not hide them away. We are the scarred steel angels of God's kingdom.

And so we need not be embarrassed about, or try to ignore, the pain and suffering we've been through. Physical or emotional scars may change us, but they certainly don't spoil us. Jesus calls us simply to be ourselves and allow these scars to show that there can be joy after pain, to show that God's peace can offer healing at even the most difficult times, and to show that Easter Sunday does follow Good Friday and Holy Saturday. 'Out of suffering have emerged the strongest souls,' writes Kahlil Gibran. 'The most massive characters are seared with scars.'

Reflection

A prayer to be prayed slowly and mindfully – allow each word and phrase to inspire your walk with God:

Lord of life,
on this Holy Saturday we bring to you everything we've been
     through in the past,
all the struggles, grief, pain, loss, disappointment and suffering.
We thank you that you redeem events and situations,
we thank you that you use each and every one of us as we are,
     whatever we have faced in the past or are going through now,
     however seared with scars we are, to help your kingdom of love
     grow and thrive.
In Jesus' name,
Amen

═══ **CONCLUSION** ═══

Open our world to your hope

Easter Sunday

The power of hope

Early on the first day of the week, while it was still dark, Mary
Magdalene went to the tomb and saw that the stone had been
removed from the entrance. So she came running to Simon
Peter and the other disciple, the one Jesus loved, and said,
'They have taken the Lord out of the tomb, and we don't know
where they have put him!'
So Peter and the other disciple started for the tomb. Both
were running, but the other disciple outran Peter and reached
the tomb first. He bent over and looked in at the strips of linen
lying there but did not go in. Then Simon Peter came along
behind him and went straight into the tomb. He saw the strips
of linen lying there, as well as the cloth that had been wrapped
round Jesus' head. The cloth was still lying in its place, separate from the linen. Finally the other disciple, who had reached
the tomb first, also went inside. He saw and believed.

JOHN 20:1–8

In the Russian Orthodox classic text *The Way of a Pilgrim*, we share the
travels of a lowly, homeless pilgrim wandering around Russia. At one
point he is mugged and robbed by two former soldiers. All he has in his
rucksack are a Bible and a book of prayers, so they are taken from him.
He's completely distraught – he feels as if he's lost the most precious
treasure possible. Later, when he is finally reunited with his books, he
hugs them to his chest and grips them so hard that his fingers lock in
place around them.

Reading this episode got me thinking what possessions would make
us distraught if they were taken from us? What would we be delighted
to be reunited with after they were stolen from us? Most of us would
not immediately think about profound spiritual and theological

objects. Perhaps we would think of our iPhones, wallets or car keys. Or perhaps we would consider some items that have sentimental value, like photographs or a gift from a loved one. For the pilgrim, though, it was not monetary or sentimental value that mattered. Rather, it was the fact these books were feeding his soul. So the challenge of *The Way of a Pilgrim* is to ask what is feeding our minds, hearts and souls?

The answer to that question lies at the heart of the event detailed in today's passage – Jesus' glorious resurrection. The group of down-hearted and dejected disciples, however, are not transformed simply· by an event; they are transformed by what that event signified in their lives. And, indeed, it still means the same for our lives today. The resurrection carries a message that can turn this world upside down and inside out – a message about faith, love and, most of all, hope.

We live in a world that tells us that material things will feed us and bring us the fulfilment, happiness and joy we long for. We place our hope in possessions, relationships, fame, wealth, pleasure and popularity. But both spiritual writers and psychologists teach us that clamouring for such things will always lead to dissatisfaction and disappointment; we will always feel that other people have more than us and we will always want more. The psychologist Oliver James refers to a strange paradox of modern life that he calls 'affluenza' – the more we have, the more we want and the unhappier we become. 'Affluenza' – our affluence is making us ill.

In the film *The Matrix* (1999) people live in a false computer-generated world. Most of them don't realise they are living a lie, but the few that do realise this decide to break out to find reality. That's what Jesus challenges us to do in this world – break out of our false way of thinking.

The Jesuit writer Anthony de Mello tells an Eastern tale of a crow who flies into the sky with a piece of bread in its beak. Twenty seagulls begin to attack him viciously, and, at first, he manages to keep hold of the bread. He flies on and fights more with the seagulls, while still grasping the bread in his bill. Finally, it is all too much and he gives in and drops the bread. As he does, all the seagulls follow the bread down, shrieking as they dive. Instead of being upset, though, the crow suddenly feels fulfilled and uplifted. He says to himself, 'I might have lost the bread, but I've gained this peaceful sky.' Many of us are so busy fighting for the bread that we don't realise that true hope is not to be found in doing, having or wanting. Rather, it's found by letting go of things. As the 14th-century theologian Meister Eckhart suggested, 'We don't find God by adding anything to our soul; no – we find God by taking things away.'

Some time ago, before I underwent a major operation on my back, I went through six months of physical pain and emotional anxiety. What was the one thing to which I clung when I went through this period of suffering? It was certainly not a material possession as such – my pain had robbed me of enjoyment of 'things' and had led me away from the false reality that had taught me that 'things' matter. It was only a small wooden cross, which I carried around at all times, that lifted my spirits, brought me peace and gave me hope.

My hope was centred upon that cross not because it was a 'thing', but because of what it represented. It was not a crucifix; it was an empty cross. In the empty cross, and in the empty tomb in today's passage, we are promised that death is not the end. Rather, the resurrection assures us that death itself is conquered. That's obviously good news for us in the future, but eternal life also has huge implications for our lives *now* – it helps us to put everything in perspective and helps us to realise that life is not about an abundance of material 'things'.

The great medieval theologian Thomas Aquinas late in his life was in a church in Naples when, suddenly, a crucifix began to speak to him. 'You have written well of me, Thomas,' Jesus said. 'Now, what reward can I give you?' To this grand question, Thomas answered, 'Non nisi te, Domine' ('None other than you, Lord'). Aquinas knew that this was the only way to find hope and fulfilment. It is not that wealth, pleasure, power, relationships and popularity are intrinsically bad – all of them can actually be used for great good. *But* we should never put our hope in them. All the things that we convince ourselves that we can't live without fade into nothing in light of the empty cross. As the famous hymn puts it, 'All my hope on God is founded.' The hymn writer did not write that some of our hope on God is founded, alongside our worldly hopes of popularity, relationships, wealth and power. No – he wrote that 'all my hope on God is founded'. Hope is to be found in letting go of the things we think are important to us, looking at the empty cross and then being inspired by that hope to live out his kingdom of love, peace and compassion in our everyday lives.

Reflection

Be truthful with yourself while you consider what possessions would make you distraught if they were lost or taken from you? A friend of mine once told me that rather than us possessing our possessions, they too often come to possess us.

Take some quiet time to close your eyes and picture yourself shedding and laying down the weighty baggage of your possessions. Now picture an empty cross, the sign of hope, peace and resurrection – and the one thing that we need to hold on to and be inspired by. Spend some time in silence and in gratitude as you imagine yourself sitting at the foot of that empty cross.

To finish, commit yourself to continue opening your life to God's kingdom and living out his hope in your everyday life by once again praying our Lenten prayer:

Loving God,
in our sufferings and joys,
in our relationships and daily lives,
we ask that your kingdom come.
Open our eyes to your presence,
open our ears to your call,
open our hearts to your love,
open our ways to your will,
open our actions to your compassion,
open our pain to your peace,
and, in doing so, open our world to your hope.
In the name of Jesus,
Amen.

Using this book in a group

While this book has principally been written for individuals, it can also be used by small groups. Group members are advised to follow individually the readings and reflections each day, then come together each week to share and discuss their thoughts and contemplations. To stimulate group discussion, the questions below are based on each week's readings. There are also suggestions for prayers at each week's meeting. You might finish each meeting by one person reading aloud, slowly and prayerfully, the prayer that sums up the journey we are taken together through Lent:

Loving God,
in our sufferings and joys,
in our relationships and daily lives,
we ask that your kingdom come.
Open our eyes to your presence,
open our ears to your call,
open our hearts to your love,
open our ways to your will,
open our actions to your compassion,
open our pain to your peace,
and, in doing so, open our world to your hope.
In the name of Jesus,
Amen

Week 1: Open our eyes to your presence

1   How can we ensure that we find time and space for God over Lent?
Share how each of you is going to take moments over the Lenten
period to slow down the pace of life to allow you to notice God's
presence.

2   Many of us have one place where we feel particularly close to God.
Where is that place for you? Explain to the group why this particular place is special to you and why you can connect with God's
presence there.

3   Where do you find that God's presence comes to you most naturally and frequently? It might be through nature, family, laughter,
music, memories, food, film or friends. Describe an event or setting that inspired you and brought you joy.

4   When do you each find God is most close to you – in times of joy or
in periods of suffering? Or perhaps in the in-between times? Think
of how we might ensure that we recognise God's presence at all
times, whatever is going on in our lives.

For prayer

Pray that we recognise God's presence over Lent – in the people we
will see, in the places we visit, in the moments of joy or fun, and in the
instances of seriousness or silence. However busy we are going to be
and however challenging the situations that we may face, we ask God
to reveal his kingdom to us over Lent.

Week 2: Open our ears to your call

1 The more we get to know someone, the more we can recognise our shared humanity and carry out our call to recognise Christ in ourselves and in each other. Take some time to get to know each other further – each of you could share a couple of facts about yourselves that others in the group might not know and then see where the conversation leads.

2 What do you enjoy doing that might be seen as a God-given talent or gift? How could you offer this for God's glory in this world? Remember that these need not be big and obvious talents, but could be smaller and more subtle ones that bring just a little light into people's lives.

3 How difficult is it to wear 'Christ spectacles' and so recognise Jesus himself in the people we meet? Consider why many of us find this to be so challenging.

4 How different is the way the contemporary world views talent and fame compared with the way Jesus lived? Think of what we can do (or, indeed, what we can avoid doing) to follow his example and not buy in to the prevalent attitudes about what makes people important and worthwhile.

For prayer

Thank God for how he calls us to live out our vocations so as to allow Jesus' light to shine in our communities. Ask that God gives opportunities for us to continue to use our gifts and talents for his praise and glory. Finally, pray that we live out our kingdom call to be Jesus to others and to see Jesus in others, whoever they may be.

Week 3: Open our hearts to your love

1   Why do you think it is hard for some people to accept God's love? Consider how we might help others to recognise how much God loves them.

2   How important do you think servanthood should be in our faith? Talk about the little things that you do in your day-to-day lives to follow Jesus' example and to live out his kingdom.

3   Share how God's love has strengthened and sustained you through difficult times in your lives – for example, you might want to consider how God gave you hope during the initial lockdown of the pandemic. How can your own experiences of God at such times help others who are going through times of trouble?

4   Consider some random acts of kindness, however small, that you could do in the run-up to Easter. Are there some things that we could all commit to do over the next few weeks?

For prayer

Pray that each and every one of us truly recognises the love God has for us and that we treat others in the light of that liberating knowledge. Ask that God helps us recognise those moments in life when we can share his love with others, even in some small, seemingly insignificant ways.

Week 4: Open our ways to your will

1 How might we ascertain what is 'God's will'? Is it possible to be certain as to what it is? Consider how we might recognise, as best we can, God's will in our lives.

2 In what ways do you feel that God communicates with you? Share ways that you ensure you are open to hearing God's voice in the cacophony of your daily lives.

3 Share with others any times in your life, or decisions you faced, when you felt a deep sense of God's will. What difference did it make in your own life or in the lives of others?

4 Tell each other about one or two Christians who were influential in your own faith journeys, either people who you knew personally or people you might have heard or read about. Once everyone has contributed, consider the differences between the people that you have mentioned with regards to tradition, age, gender, background and so on.

For prayer

Pray that we are open to recognising, and then listening to, God's will in our lives. Ask that Jesus guides us and transforms us into his image, so that we can reflect his kingdom and become blessings in the faith journeys of others, just as others have been so inspirational in our own journeys.

Week 5: Open our actions to your compassion

1 Share examples of when you have seen or experienced compassion being carried out. You might want to consider, for example, times during the pandemic when you saw people live out compassion. In light of your discussion, how can you put compassion into action in your own daily lives?

2 Imagine if the story of the compassionate Samaritan were retold today. Who might be seen as today's Samaritans and who might be seen as the priests and Levites? The Samaritan risked his life to help – how difficult is it for us to live in this way? Consider how compassion might demand that we are prepared to sacrifice or that we go beyond our comfort zone.

3 In what ways can we carry out the biblical imperative to care for the environment? Discuss steps we could take over Lent and beyond to ensure we damage our environment as little as possible.

4 'The compassion-filled value system of the kingdom of God subverts the value system of the kingdoms of money, prestige and power.' Take time to consider this sentence. What is it saying? Do you agree with it? How can we ensure that we prioritise compassion over other competing values?

For prayer

Ask that God, *our* Father, helps us to see others, however different they may be from us, as our brothers and sisters. Pray that we realign our priorities so that we live kingdom lives of compassion, showing care and love to other people, other living things and the environment around us.

Week 6: Open our pain to your peace

1 How difficult is it to trust God when we are going through a time of darkness? Share with the group moments when you have trusted him through a period of pain or suffering or have witnessed others do so.

2 Have there been times in your lives when illness, stress, fear or worry seemed too much to cope with? Were you able to find any comfort, peace or reassurance in your situation? If so, from where did that come?

3 Has God ever seemed silent, or even absent, in your life? Consider the idea that prayer might include the whole range of human emotions, including anger, frustration and protest. How can the Bible help us when we feel this way? Are there particular books or characters that might give us comfort, reassurance or inspiration?

4 Consider as a group the idea that our scars, physical and emotional, are the things that make us who we are and can become a gift to others who are going through difficulties. What are your scars? How has God redeemed them and how do they now bear witness to his kingdom?

For prayer

Pray for the light of Christ to shine where there is pain and suffering in our lives, and pray for peace and healing for any past suffering that still has a hold on us. Ask for God's blessing on our lives, and ask that he helps us to trust him in any difficulties or challenges we face on our journeys.

Week 7: Beyond Easter
Open our world to your hope

You might want to meet again as a group after Easter, to consider the importance of the resurrection and to reflect on your Lenten journey together. Here are some questions to aid your discussion:

1 Share words that you associate with Easter. What are the things that are important to you and your faith about Easter?

2 Take turns to each share a joyful memory in your past – when was it? Who did you share it with? What happened? In what way did it give you hope? How can it inspire your present and future?

3 Where do you find hope in today's world? Consider where Christians can see signs of new life and resurrection in the world and in their lives.

4 What have been the most helpful and hopeful insights that you have gained from the group discussions over Lent? What will you take away and cherish?

For prayer

Pray that opening ourselves to God's kingdom helps us to share the hope, resurrection and new life of Easter with others. Ask God to bring light into the darkness that people face, hope into the hopelessness that many feel and joy into the temptation to be cynical or grow weary.

Bibliography

Many of the quotations and references I have used in this book have been collected over many years from films, books, newspapers, music lyrics, reliable internet sources and television programmes. However, to give readers the opportunity to explore topics further, I include here a bibliography of the principal texts that were used in the writing of the book.

Karen Armstrong, *Twelve Steps to a Compassionate Life* (Bodley Head, 2011).

Robert Barron, *Thomas Aquinas: Spiritual master* (Crossroad, 2008).

Robert Barron, *To Light a Fire on the Earth: Proclaiming the gospel in a secular age* (Image, 2017).

Karl Barth, *Church Dogmatics, Volume IV.I: The doctrine of reconciliation* (T and T Clark, 1956).

William Blake, *The Complete Poems* (Penguin, 2004).

Dietrich Bonhoeffer, *Life Together* (SCM, 1992).

Dietrich Bonhoeffer, *The Cost of Discipleship* (SCM, 2001).

Joseph Campbell, *The Hero with a Thousand Faces* (New World Library, 2012).

G.K. Chesterton, *Orthodoxy* (Cavalier Books, 2015).

Joan Chittister, *Joan Chittister: Essential writings* (Orbis, 2014).

Charles de Foucauld, *Charles de Foucauld: Essential writings* (Orbis, 1999).

Anthony de Mello, *The Song of the Bird* (Doubleday, 1984).

Anthony de Mello, *Awareness* (Fount, 1997).

Anthony de Mello, *The Way to Love: Meditations for life* (Random House, 2012).

Danny Dorling, *Injustice: Why social inequality still persists* (Policy Press, 2015).

Meister Eckhart, *Selected Writings* (Penguin, 1994).

Loren Eiseley, *The Star Thrower* (Harvest, 1979).

T.S. Eliot, *Collected Poems 1909–62* (Faber and Faber, 2002).

Jack D. Forbes, *Columbus and Other Cannibals: The wetiko disease of exploitation, imperialism, and terrorism* (Seven Stories Press, 2008).

Richard J. Foster and James Bryan Smith (eds), *Devotional Classics: Selected readings for individuals and groups* (Hodder and Stoughton, 2003).

Viktor Frankl, *Man's Search For Meaning: The classic tribute to hope from the Holocaust* (Rider, 2004).

Neil Gaiman, *American Gods* (Headline, 2017).

Keith Hebden, *Re-enchanting the Activist: Spirituality and social change* (Jessica Kingsley, 2017).

Trystan Owain Hughes, *Finding Hope and Meaning in Suffering* (SPCK, 2010).

Trystan Owain Hughes, *Real God in the Real World: Advent and Christmas readings on the coming of Christ* (BRF, 2013).

Trystan Owain Hughes, *The Compassion Quest* (SPCK, 2013).

Trystan Owain Hughes, *Living the Prayer: The everyday challenge of the Lord's Prayer* (BRF, 2017).

Trystan Owain Hughes, *Winds of Change: The Roman Catholic Church and society in Wales 1916–62* (University of Wales Press, 2017).

Oliver James, *Affluenza* (Vermilion, 2007).

Andrew Jones, *Pilgrimage: The journey to remembering our story* (BRF, 2011).

Mark Kermode, *The Good, the Bad and the Multiplex* (Arrow, 2012).

Amy-Jill Levine and Marc Zvi Brettler (eds), *The Jewish Annotated New Testament* (OUP, 2011).

C.S. Lewis, *Surprised by Joy* (Fount, 1998).

C.S. Lewis, *Weight of Glory: And other addresses* (Zondervan, 2001).

C.S. Lewis, *Screwtape Letters: Letters from a senior to a junior devil* (Collins, 2016).

Robert MacFarlane, *The Old Ways: A journey on foot* (Penguin, 2013).

Alister McGrath, *Christian Theology: An introduction* (Blackwell, 2001).

Brennan Manning, *The Ragamuffin Gospel* (Authentic, 2009).

Thomas Merton, *Seasons of Celebration: Meditations on the cycle of liturgical feasts* (Farrar, Straus and Giroux, 1965).

Thomas Merton, *Thomas Merton: Essential writings* (Orbis, 2000).

Andy Miller, *The Kinks Are the Village Green Preservation Society: 33 1/3* (Continuum, 2010).

Gordon Mursell, *Out of the Deep: Prayer as protest* (DLT, 1989).

John Henry Newman, *Essay in Aid of a Grammar of Assent* (University of Notre Dame Press, 1979).

James O'Brien, *How To Be Right: In a world gone wrong* (Penguin, 2019).

Edward T. Oakes and David Moss (eds), *The Cambridge Companion to Hans Urs von Balthasar* (CUP, 2009).

George Orwell, *The Lion and the Unicorn: Socialism and the English genius* (Penguin, 2018).

R.J. Palacio, *Wonder* (Random House, 2014).

R. Williams Parry, *Cerddi R. Williams Parry: Y Casgliad Cyflawn* (Gwasg Gee, 1998).

Mike Pilavachi, *Wasteland? Encountering God in the desert* (Kingsway, 2003).

Richard Rees, *Simone Weil: A sketch for a portrait* (OUP, 1966).

Michael Rosen, *We're Going on a Bear Hunt* (Walker Books, 1993).

E.F. Schumacher, *A Guide for the Perplexed* (Vintage, 1995).

Albert Schweitzer, *Albert Schweitzer: Essential writings* (Orbis, 2005).

Magdalen Smith, *Steel Angels: The personal qualities of a priest* (SPCK, 2014).

Dorothee Soelle, *Dorothee Soelle: Essential writings* (Orbis, 2006).

The Green Bible: A priceless message that doesn't cost the earth (Collins, 2008).

The Jewish Study Bible (OUP, 2014).

The Way of a Pilgrim and The Pilgrim Continues His Way (Image, 2003).

Mark Thibodeaux, *Reimagining the Ignatian Examen: Fresh ways to pray from your day* (Loyola Press, 2015).

R.S. Thomas, *Collected Poems: 1945–1990* (Phoenix, 1993).

Henry David Thoreau, *Walden; or Life in the Woods* (Dover, 1995).

Phyllis Tickle, *Phyllis Tickle: Essential spiritual writings* (Orbis, 2015).

Desmond Tutu, *God Has a Dream: A vision of hope for our time* (Rider, 2004).

Miroslav Volf, *A Public Faith: How followers of Christ should serve the common good* (Brazos Press, 2011).

Richard Wilkinson and Kate Pickett, *The Spirit Level: Why equality is better for everyone* (Penguin, 2010).

Philip Yancey, *What's so Amazing about Grace? Visual edition* (Zondervan, 2003).

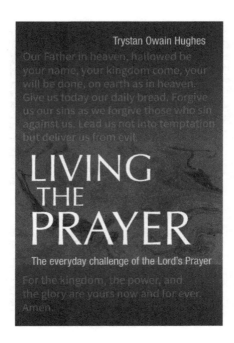

What are we really saying when we say the Lord's Prayer? What are we expecting? *Living the Prayer* is a fresh perspective on the Lord's Prayer. Rooted in the Bible as well as in contemporary culture, it explores how this prayer can radically challenge and transform our daily lives. Contained in the prayer's 70 words is a fresh and innovative way of viewing, and acting in, the world that is as relevant now as it was 2,000 years ago. The author shows that this revolutionary prayer demands that we don't remain on our knees, but, rather, that we work towards making God's topsy-turvy, downside-up kingdom an everyday reality.

Living the Prayer
The everyday challenge of the Lord's Prayer
Trystan Owain Hughes
978 0 85746 623 5 £7.99

brfonline.org.uk

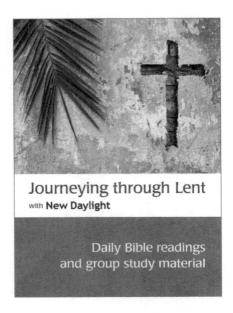

Journeying through Lent
with **New Daylight**

Daily Bible readings
and group study material

This resource provides Lent material at an affordable price, using material by well-loved contributors from the *New Daylight* archive alongside specially written questions for group discussion. It encourages groups and individuals, whether existing readers of *New Daylight* or those who are new to using Bible reading notes, to share their experience and reflect together on the Lent journey as a church community.

Journeying through Lent with New Daylight
Daily Bible readings and group study material
Edited by Sally Welch
978 0 85746 965 6 £2.99

brfonline.org.uk

Enabling all ages to grow in faith

Anna Chaplaincy
Living Faith
Messy Church
Parenting for Faith

The Bible Reading Fellowship (BRF) is a Christian charity that resources individuals and churches. Our vision is to enable people of all ages to grow in faith and understanding of the Bible and to see more people equipped to exercise their gifts in leadership and ministry.

To find out more about our ministries, visit
brf.org.uk

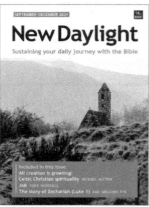

New Daylight provides four months of daily Bible readings and comment, with a regular team of contributors drawn from a range of church backgrounds. It is ideal for anybody wanting an accessible yet stimulating aid to spending time with God each day, deepening their faith and their knowledge of scripture.

New Daylight
Sustaining your daily journey with the Bible
Edited by Sally Welch

brfonline.org.uk/new-daylight